ONOMATOPEE 44

Abecedarium
[A Former Fragment]

BY

JOHN C. WELCHMAN

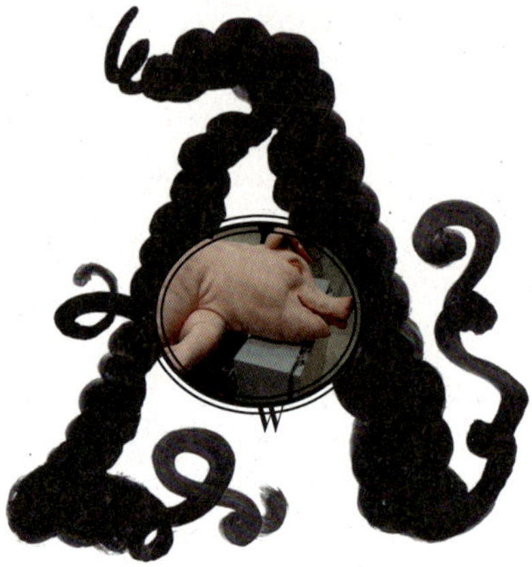

ANIMATRONICS

The move of *Giantbum* from setting to set traces a wider shift from the era of human-spirit compounds (saints, icons, angels, demons, ghouls and ghosts) to regimes of mechanical supplementation or the replacement of the human body and its functions (automata, robots, cyborgs, animatrons). As the most recent and commercially viable of these mecanomorphic devices, much of the utopian allure attaching to earlier compounds of human (or animal) and machine has been stripped from the making, use and reception of animatronic objects. Largely the product of innovations in the Hollywood design apparatus, their value lies in a camera-ready capacity for pure simulation down to the level of micro-movements (breathing, blinking, smiling) allied to the fabrication of identikit surfaces (skin, faces, hair and fur).

As animatronic technologies passed into the art world their primary concentration on simulated effects gave way to various disruptions of the complicity with truth they purportedly engendered. In the work of Paul MCCARTHY, for example, the retreat from similitude developed along two parallel tracks. Not only—first of all—were his earlier animatronic devices somewhat crude and disjunctive at the mechanical level, somewhat in step with the development of the technology itself, but at the same time they were used to stage repetitive acts of an unseemly nature, such as the man humping a tree in *The Garden* (1991-92). Unseemly, but also unseen, for McCarthy put animatronics to work against the grain of its happily prurient visibility. In later pieces such as *Caribbean Pirates* (2001-2005), secondly, McCarthy went so far as to commission several elaborate animatronic pieces, including a Captain Morgan head and an animatronic pig, which, in the end, he barely used (reserving the latter for a work-in-progress, *Pig Island*).

Mellors picks up where McCarthy left off, and at the same time inflects this legacy in several dimensions. He has subjected machines that duplicate and repeat to new rounds of repetition and duplication in the disturbingly homogenous trio of faces modelled after the visage of actor Johnny Vivash who plays The Father. Then he unstitches the heads from their formal completion, exposing the mechanical and electrical elements in the backs of their heads, thus producing an aberrant—and finally impossible—form of quasi-simulation. Finally, he re-calibrates the larger genealogy of human and animular compounds by firing up his unholy Trinity in the space between spiritual and physical worlds, which they occupy with a weave of uncanny mannerism and manic dissimulation.

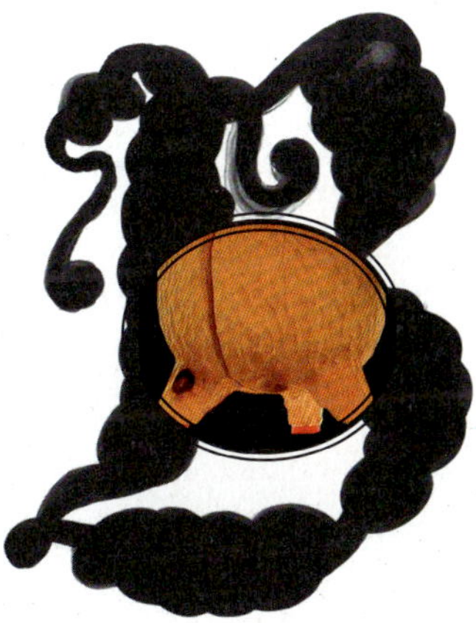

BORN-AGAIN

One of the clearest of the many recursive structures that underpin the speculative logic of *Giantbum* is the persistent presence of the pseudo-evangelical trope of a body 'born-again'. The central proposition here turns on the cyclical exchange between consumption, evacuation and recomposition—or the poop loop. In the crucial moment of this reflux, The Father makes note of his own transubstantiation, that his being has been 'much changed': 'I have been...born-again—you may not recognise me. I have become—something else. In this Giant's lower intestine—I became—something else.' Sir Boss delivers an exegetical commentary on the implications of all this when he 'fears' that 'The Father's diet has seen him give birth to himself.' To which The Truthcurator retorts: 'You mean he's been born again?'

Like an extra-long dining table, the strain of revivification thus engendered has several leaves. While one is predicated on out-and-out bestiality, the hybrid 'monstrosity' of The Father's adopted body parts, especially his 'shitty', 'rubbishy' arms, is not simply the product of their excremental composition. It is, rather, a function of a new relativity in the concept of 'truth', so that, as Sir Boss has it, The Father 'is being sculptural with the truth.' The make-up of this para-sculptural activity is dependent on two functions—auto-production (which is to say, along with Sir Boss, that The Father 'has *regenerated* himself'); and at the same time a material incrementality, a certain piecemeal bit-by-bitness that gives rise to the process of being 'born again...in small stages'.

A second leaf arrives in the form of Mellors' theological bathos. The experience of being born-again is modelled on a connective chain of redemptive opportunities, for

> 'Just as God *re-launched* himself as Jesus as a sort of 'second chance' for all those who had ignored him, so Jesus, now, in His *empathy* for our condition has modernised himself—INTO SOME POO!'

If there is any resolution to this spiritual diminuendo it will arise from nominalist revision, so that The Father has to be renamed, beginning with the designation , 'Rather-More-Than-Father' (*see* **FATHER**).

These splits and extensions lead the new slate of religious reaffirmation through a coprophagous detour as the self declares its alliance with the transcendence of divine singularity by taking up with its own number two. Add them together (*see* **NUMEROLOGY**), with a clause for sitting, and Mellors' heretical Trinitarianism is one and the same as a three-legged stool.

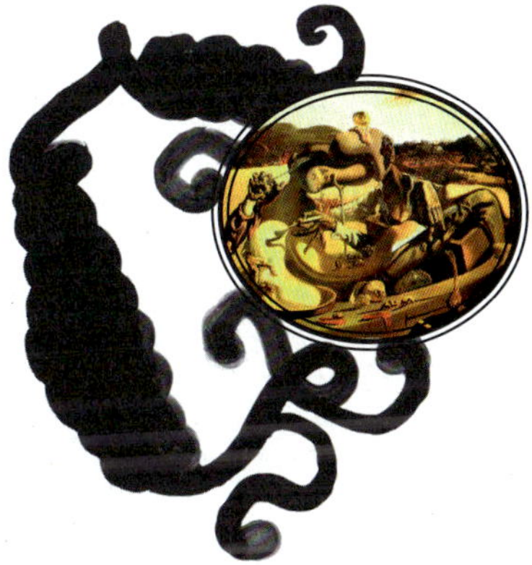

CANNIBALISM

Mellors' disquisition on cannibalistic consumption is posed, like that of Salvador Dalí, in relation to the theological mysticism of the Eucharist; but it functions somewhat as the reverse (and inverse) of a construction that is already done ass-backwards. In 'les caprices pincés princiers', the first section of *Les dîners de Gala* (1973), Dalí meditates on the 'sado-masochistic pleasure' of eating 'cooked and living beings' (a tradition he ascribes to 'the Neapolitan, of Catalan descent, Giambattista della Porta'—a noted physiognomist, *see* **OUTSIDE**). Here Dalí finds a 'gastronomic confirmation' 'of our Catholic, Apostolic and Roman Rumanian Religion, i.e; to swallow the living God as is done in the Sacrament of the Eucharist.'[1] Cannibalistic consumption, the ingestion of one's own kind, functions almost continuously for Dalí as the inevitable death-driven obverse to the notion of eating as healthy consumption. Alongside and in competition with the normative itinerary of food—starting with natural display and confected culinary reordering (preparation, recipes, menus), using the face as its entryway, the stomach as a locus of digestive incorporation and the bowels as an exit for the precipitation of surplus—Dalí sets up a counter-logic of putrefaction, cannibalism and death.

Dalían cannibalism is part of the wider agenda of his theory of 'critical paranoia' according to which things in the visible world conspire to consume those who look at them. In Dalí's formulation, architecture, especially what he termed 'the terrifying and edible beauty of [Antoni Gaudí's] Art Nouveau architecture', must be rendered sublimely digestible and subject to the implications of a 'new Surrealist age of "the cannibalism of objects."'[2]

In *Giantbum*, Mellors puts all this in colossal parentheses that he bends around the corners of the past and then along the edges of the future. On the one hand, an allegorically huge object (the giant) has already swallowed the explorers so that what unfolds inside its belly is a meta-cannibalistic event that takes place in the aftermath of a prior act of (albeit involuntary) cannibalism. On the other, we are strategically stationed at the historical threshold of the sacramental discourse of transubstantiation, that mysterious transformation of the physical constituency of bread and wine into flesh and blood, one of the first articulations of which was made at the Fourth Lateran Council of 1215.

DATE

1213. As if cast out from a heretical Fibonacci sequence, Mellors' *numerus typicus* might posit the apostles plus their Great Leader; thus serving as a code-number for the occult rationalism of the sacraments.

The first degree-granting universities in Europe were founded in this era (Bologna, 1088; Paris, c. 1150; Oxford, 1167; Cambridge, 1209; Salamanca, 1218; Montpellier, 1220; Padua, 1222; Naples, 1224; Toulouse, 1229), which is coterminous with the rise of scholasticism and the codification of both Common and Canon Law.

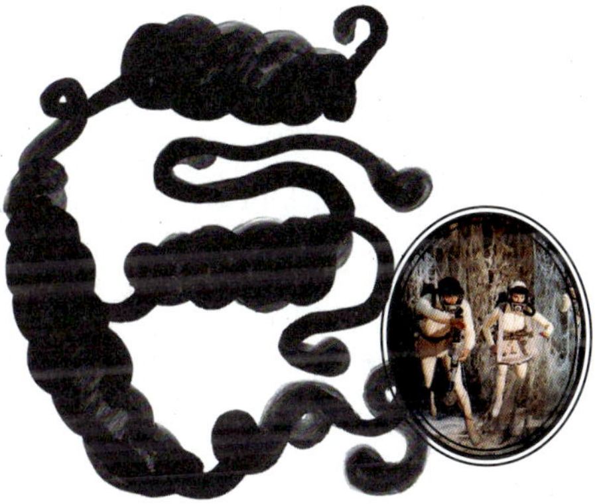

EXPLORATION

The expeditionary quotient of Mellors' project is fuelled by a genealogy that includes, in and around the art world, the Dakar-Djibouti expedition undertaken by students of Marcel Mauss between 1931 and 1933 and featured in the second issue of *Minotaure*; Mike Kelley's prurient spelunkers and his general subterranean obsessions; and the tragic aesthetic Columbianism of Bas Jan Ader. Mellors heads inwards of course, on a fictive itinerary aligned more with the popular sci-fi legacies of the *Journey to the Center of the Earth* (Jules Verne, 1864) or the lineage of Hollywood shrink flicks from *The Incredible Shrinking Man* (dir. Jack Arnold, 1957) and the *Fantastic Voyage* (dir. Richard Fleischer, 1966) to *Honey, I Shrunk the Kids* (dir. Joe Johnston, 1989) and National Geographic's *Inside the Living Body* (dir. Martin Williams, 2007). All this is then lightly infested by the survivalist paradigms of live-action and reality TV as set out in *Lost* (2004-10) and *Survivor* (2000-), before being supersaturated with linguistic adrenaline in another rewind of the Holy Grail (sanguine on hold).

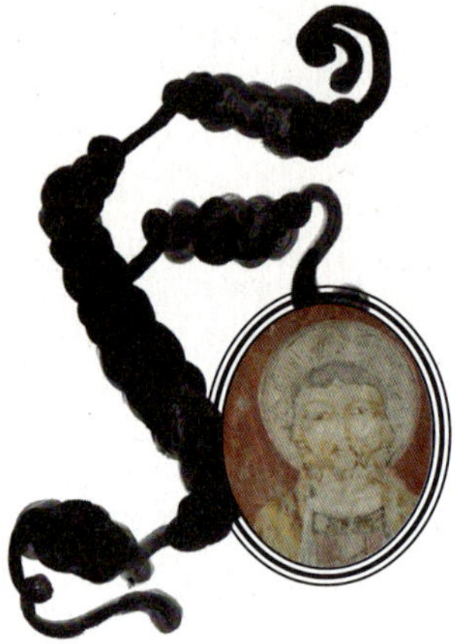

FATHER, THE

Aka Rather-More-Than Father; The Father and loam; Peasant and strip; Father Plus; Father Father; Doctor Poo; The Landlord and the pub; Father Shitmass. Fixed with symbolic indistinction somewhere between Our Father and an alehouse Oedipus Rex the eponymous patronymic that intermittently governs the action in *Giantbum* is a febrile allegory of the Law... though without certified jurisdiction or proper tribunal. We might think of him, in fact, as a cipher for the Common Law, or as a mode of becoming for the case-based reasoning, known as casuistry that emerged in 12th and 13th century England immediately before and after the formalisation of Common Law by Henry II in 1154.

The Father's rather glutinous authority seems predicated on an agglomeration of incidents and experiences rationalised by an off-stage logic that masquerades as the commencement of civic society. The Father offers a review of these developments caught in reverse, like precedent seen through a rearview mirror. This might account for the incessant supplementarity of The Father's nomination, his Rather-More-Than-Fatherhood. For he is a superconductor between family and land, overlordship and tenancy, Higher Power and excremental remnants. He makes pantomimic common cause with the syntagmatic temporality of Common Law, parodying its gradual accumulation of precedents and centralising ambition to wean the juridical scene from the burdens of locality (*see* **TERRITORIALITY**).

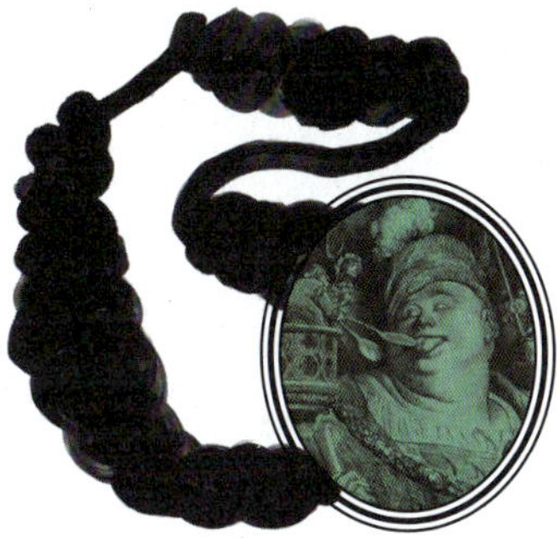

***GARGANTUA AND OF PANTAGRUEL, THE LIFE OF* (1532-64)**

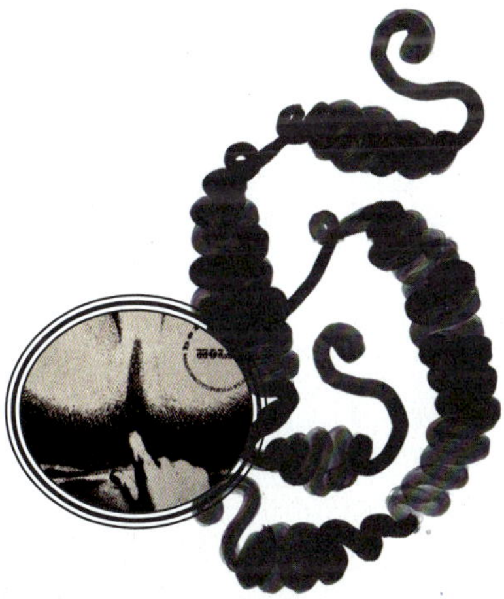

HUMOR

With exception of YELLOW, there are few traces here of the primary colors of the medieval humors: phlegmatic green; sanguine red; and bilious blue. Blacker than André Breton's 'humor noire' and diffidently bluer than common smut, the comedic spectrum of *Giantbum* is fundamentally brown.[3]

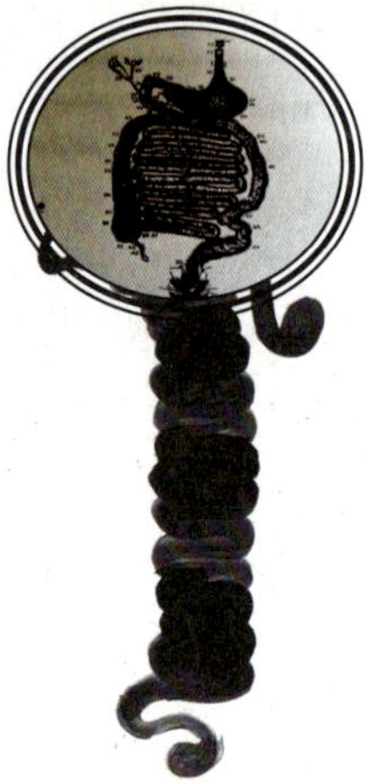

INTESTINES (*see* VISCERA)

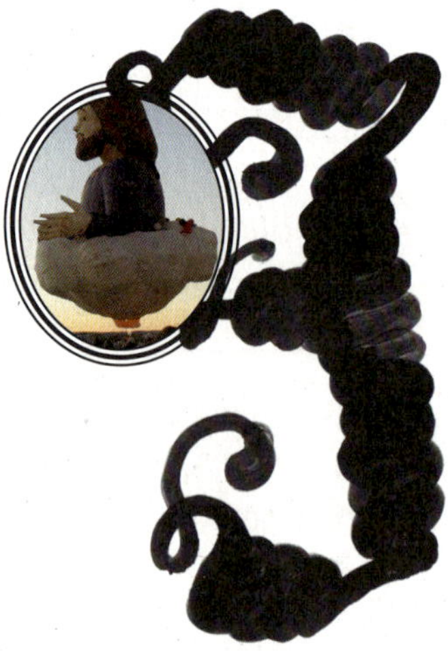

JESUS (*see* BORN-AGAIN)

In Mellors' dissident christology, Jesus is a modernised modification of God in the form of poo, otherwise known as the 'gynaecologist of God's bum'.

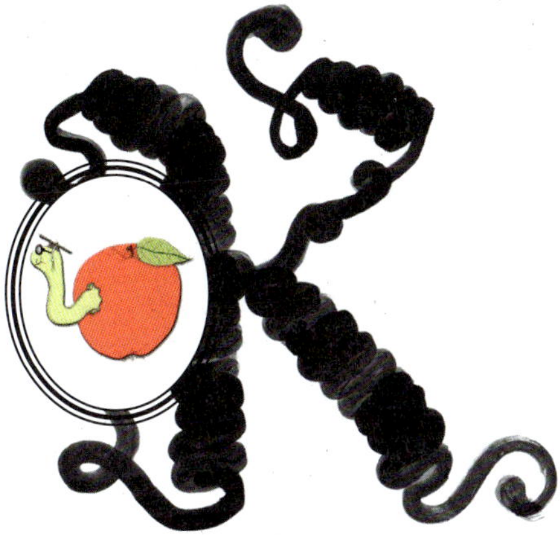

KNOWLEDGE

Not much is actually known, or even claimed to be known, or found out, in *Giantbum* as internalisation and cyclical repetition give rise to an epistemological wasteland. In the zonal marking system prevalent in the gut, crosses bearing marks of the truth get nudged away for corners, only to be sent back again for more of the same. The players go awol and only the spaces between them seem to be inhabited—by the unstable traces they leave behind. So when Sir Boss elides the difference between 'telling' and 'knowing' in the phantom reportage of The Father on the subject of 'becoming Ploppen', he precipitates a paternal outburst that represents the script's most extravagant exclamatory rant:

> 'Arrgggggggghhhh!...Argghhhhhhfghdgghhh!...Aghhghghghghghghhhhhhhhhh!... Ngggghhhh... Godgifu! Godgyfu! Godgifu!...BRRRRPPPPPPPRRPRPPRPPRPRPRP.'

This bracketing of knowledge with expletive incontinence spills over associatively when Sir Boss offers it a climactic, punning denouement: 'Urggghhh! No! I mean—I mean I *know* I mean—I know!' Meaning, negating and knowing are simultaneously aligned and undermined here in a terrifying triple eclipse in which the nullity (*see* **ZERO**) of knowledge is the only thing that finally becomes meaning.

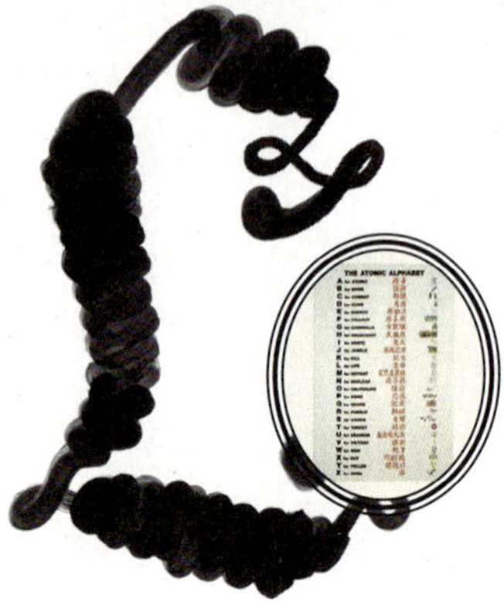

LANGUAGE (*see* SCRIPT)

Mellors has long made it clear that the playfulness, texture, excesses and other edge-conditions of language are realigned at the very the heart of his performative enterprise. While the narrative of *The Time Surgeon* (2007) 'is essentially a battle for the control of language', in *Giantbum* and other works everything that transpires is, as the artist puts it himself, 'improvised within a primarily linguistic arena'.[4] Language works here as a kind of afterburn generated at the intoxicated confluence of punning repartee, monographic free-fall and mordant dialectic.

The linguistic space opened up by Mellors is bounded by three historical deployments of language in the art world which he overlays, fools with, and finally displaces. The first arrived with the pressures of ceaseless ironisation and outright absurdity offered up by artists associated with the Dada movement in the later 1910s—a situation in which words and sounds, as Tristan Tzara wrote in 1918, are 'thrown into the air like an acoustic disc',[5] party to an uncoordinated search for 'the extreme limit of the possible divorce between words and meaning'.[6] A second horizon for the fraught relation between language and visual form in the modernist period disabuses the pretensions of semantic order in another dimension. For amidst the clamourous arguments for the discursive separation of words and images driven by the relentless pursuit of formal autonomy, language time and again broke back into the frame-bounded pictorial arena to wreak havoc with the misprision of silence it variously posited. This was manifest in relation to the 'abstract' image even before the precepts of non-iconic abstraction were fully realised in the years after 1910, witness the witty, linguistic monochromes produced by Alphonse Allais in the years around 1890, which included *Première communion de jeunes Filles chlorotiques par un Temps de Neige* (*First Communion of Anemic Young Girls in the Snow*, 1893), presented as a sheet of white Bristol paper modified only by the addition of the title and an elaborate, printed frame. At the other end of the modernist era language once again ran riot with the quiescent dictates of modernist theory as artists including Morris Louis and Anthony Caro, Frank Stella and Jules Olitski added personal, poetic, offbeat and occasionally outlandish titular supplements to their purportedly well-mannered and linguistically neutered compositions.[7]

In the heyday of all this of course, a third position emerged with the development in the late 1960s of Conceptual Art, some aspects of which attempted to redeem the implications of the first and turn the second inside out by announcing the priority of language in the name of art. Mellors reasserts the priority accorded to language by Conceptualism, but utterly disdains its unremitting seriousness and analytic dryness; he re-imagines the ribald humour and debunkery of Dada and the epic one-liners of Allais and the Salon of Incoherent Art, but transposes them into episodic narratives driven forward by concatenations of visual incident and technological addenda.

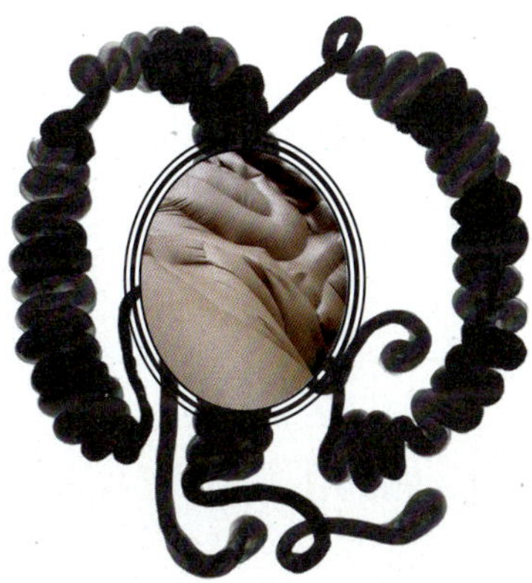

MCCARTHY, PAUL (*see* ANIMATRONICS *and* PASOLINI)

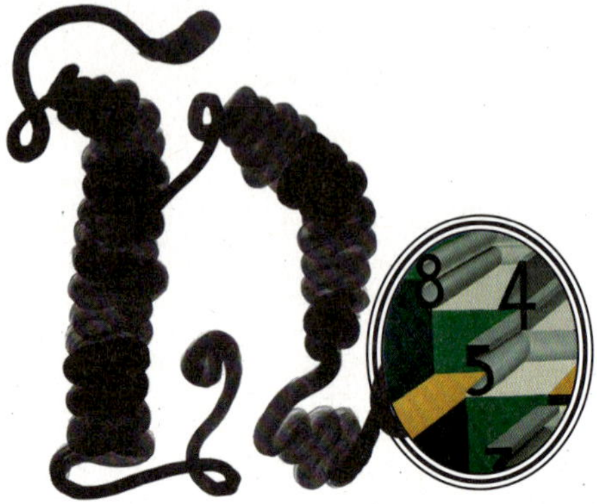

NUMEROLOGY (*see* DATE *and* ZERO)

After the date (1213) and the number designating the group (103) there are the passing days, '1!2!3!4!5!6!7!8!' that measure out the captivity of the explorers in the intestinal regions of the giant.

Then, the 'sequential aims', designed to accommodate two purposes, the maintenance of hydration and the '*idea* of escape', adumbrated by the Sub-Priest, five of them, nos. 1 through 7, but without 2 and 6. Finally we pass through The Father's 'number of unframed questions' prompted by his epiphanic revelation while posting himself in the lower bowel on avant-garde reconnaissance duty. Another 5.

Mellors' project alchemises number into *numbum*, a special discourse of numerical paralysis transacted in the nether regions. Here the artist lights a digital bonfire for the vanities of prefiguration and concurrence, fuelled by the tradition of mystical enumeration encapsulated in the *De mystica numerorum significatione* (first ed. 1583-1584) of Pietro Bongo (Petrus Bongus), which attempted to unite the mystical numerological speculations of Pythagorus with the Jewish Kabbalah and Christianity.

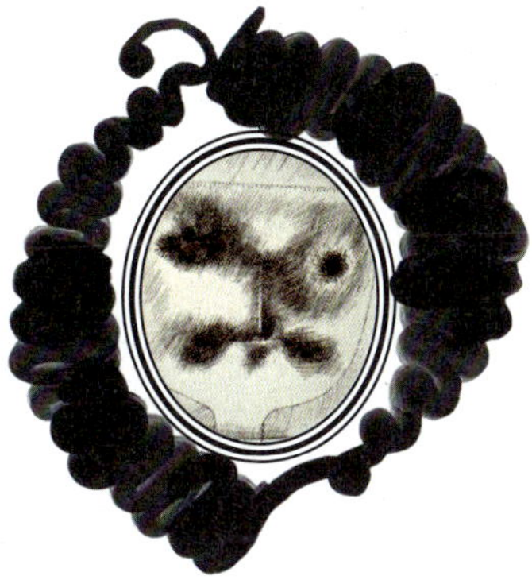

OUTSIDE

Predicated on enigmatic protocols of transference between inside and outside, the procrastinating relativities of front and behind, and various determinations of embodiment and un-incorporation, the vector system at work in *Giantbum* is a waywardly animating force that conjures up a number of evasively crucial points of view. Perhaps the governing orientation is what Sir Boss terms 'vertical logic', the directed force of up and down that simultaneously 'wows' and converts. Mellors' protagonists are, of course, prisoners inside the gravitational pull of a putatively upright body within which the un-incorporated remnants of what has been ingested move inexorably through the digestive tract, into the bowels, to be purged (or restored to the outside) in a final downward movement.

The inevitable pull of this consumptive journey reminds us of Schopenhauer's attribution of human-like feelings or sensations to the natural world in his essay, 'On the Metaphysics of Fine Art.' Here Schopenhauer surveys three dominant features of nature—its inorganic mineral or geological hardness, its organic profusion in the form of vegetation and the effects of water in a landscape—ascribing to each emotional responses that he believes to be true and universal. What he does, in effect, is to treat these types of natural environment as objects for physiognomy, inferring from them an essential character that triggers a particular human response. Bare, rocky, desert-like landscapes, such as 'that long valley of rocks… without a trace of vegetation, near Toulouse, on the way to Marseilles' or the African desert give rise to melancholy, sadness, even oppressive feelings. The reason for this, Schopenhauer asserts is that such regions 'obey only one law, the law of gravity; and consequently everything is disposed in accordance with it'.[8]

Conversely, vegetation, especially when 'rich, various, luxuriant and left to itself' confers on human spectators 'a feeling of direct pleasure'. Again, the rationale for such emotions is attributed to the effects of gravity, which in this case have been overcome by the sprouting, budding, shooting upward and sideways motion of vegetal growth. Schopenhauer proves his rule with an exception, the tree that 'bends over the earth with its branches obedient to the laws of gravity [which] makes us melancholy',[9] referring, of course, to the weeping willow, whose popular name bears with it the implications Schopenhauer defends.

The part taken by the pseudo-science of physiognomy is key not only to the causal nexus between face and mind, in particular, and surfaces and interiors in general, but offers a mode of moral accountancy and speculative analogy that shifted in the epoch between the high middle ages and early modernity from the (exterior) predicates of astral and cosmological determinism to the inscription of character and behavioural predisposition from the inside out—so that, as formalised by Johann Casper Lavater and his numerous acolytes and followers, the shapes, proportions and protruberances of faces and skulls could be decoded as the symptoms of particular forms of human nature. Mellors offers a wittily allusive inversion of all this when Sir Boss asks, in the coda beyond 'The End', whether 'God is behind…this…behind'—a proposition that confuses tops and bottoms, and like the demonological imagery of the Middle Ages, witnesses the disjunct overlay of faces on joints and genitals.

This is one measure accounting for the 'fatal' exclamations of Sir Boss following his punning proclamation on the putatively divine underpinning of *Giantbum*. The Truthcurator delivers another when he annotates the discrepant 'points of view' on offer with a proclamation on perspective:

> 'you helped me see it from your point of view. Sir Boss, what is your perspective on the ins and outs, the ups and downs, the

> horizontals and the verticals of the whole situation?'

Sir Boss retorts,

> 'My perspective is diagonal. Nonetheless since man got up from all fours he has been joined directly from arse to tit and is prone to seeing things vertically.'

The discourse on the fallibilities of exteriority that ensues is one of the pseudo-philosophical hubs of *Giantbum*. It is, of course, a riff on scholastic ruminations such as the *Summa Theologiae* of Aquinas,[10] which purport to interrogate the omnipotent totality of the divine. A later and somewhat atypical variant, Nicholas de Cusa's *The Vision of God or the Icon*, takes us back to the question of the face.[11] Here the project of seeing God in the form of an icon gives rise to a rhetorical tour de force of omnivoyance, in which, as in the parodic interiorisations of *Giantbum*, there is no exit from the principle of transcendence, no matter which way you look.

Mellors pushes the envelope of the paradoxical switch-system between 'out' and 'in' (and 'top' and—especially—'bottom'), by riffing on almost every metaphorical denomination of exteriority and its many opposites. First, the savage Ploppen are said to be guardians of the 'rear end' which they 'protect…from the inside-out!' Sir Boss, on the other hand, determines that they are the fantastical projections of The Father's deluded imagination…his desperate attempt to '*externalise* something?' Secondly, The Father's crucial round of interrogations (*see* **QUESTIONS**), begins with a literal meditation on the lost exterior—'Question 1: Why is it impossible for us to find a way out of the giant?'—which gives rise to a series of farcically literal responses, before ushering in the philosophical conundrum that lies at the heart of the performance: [Sir Boss] 'Because the giant has no perineum? Because he's just like a big pillow, with no arms or legs or holes! No—sorry—it's because he's already outside.' Or rather as The Father retorts, 'because this Giant *has no outside*!'

The properties and possibilities of a possibly phantom outside generates a crisis in 'visualisation' and literal measurement (with 'string') which is crossed with the travails of memory and belief, before a solution arrives in the form of a final omnipotence: the outside and the inside are always the same when both the place and object of speculation are nothing other than 'the bowels of—GOD!!'

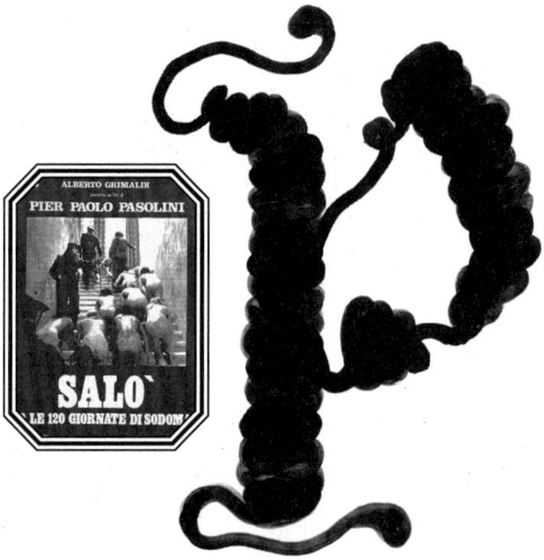

PASOLINI, PIER PAOLO

When Paul **MCCARTHY** began his own version of the 'scripting' process for *Caribbean Pirates* in 2004-05, he sent his actors home with copies of Pasolini's *Salò, or the 120 Days of Sodom* (1975) and the film version of Edward Albee's *Who's Afraid of Virginia Woolf* (1966, dir. Mike Nichols, with Elizabeth Taylor and Richard Burton) in lieu of more formalised directives. McCarthy puts his marauding methodology to work by echoing and transposing Pasolini's counter-historicisation, referential layering (the Marquis de Sade and his commentators, including Roland Barthes, Fascist erotics, etc.), and defamiliarising techniques, at the same time raising the stakes of his excremental fetishisation beyond the flashpoint of sensual indulgence.[12]

Somewhat less atavistically, Mellors too, absconds with some of the horrifying implications of Pasolini's cinema, noting that the 'idea of cannibalism and the use of coprophilia' were part of the 'considerable influence' he derived from '*Porcile* (1969) and *Salò* (1975) respectively.'

'I think *Salò*', he continued, 'is a total masterpiece, quite unlike any other film I've seen. It has a heightened sense of realism despite its lack of naturalism. Pasolini demonstrates the worst possible outcome within an environment where "the rules have changed"—there has been a deliberate disconnection from any comparative measure of reality—and he shows this as a precondition for torture and total abuse. You see that progression in *Salò*. At first people are abducted from their normal lives. That's the beginning of the slippage—it gets worse and worse. Inside the island-state into which they are abducted the languages of art and power refer only to their own art and power. Horror becomes normalised; the environment is degraded. There are many parallels that can be made between that manipulation of "the rules" and trends in our social and political environment post 9-11.'[13]

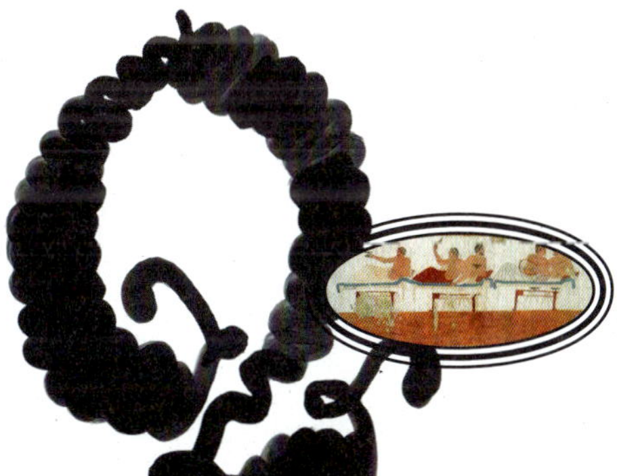

Q & A

The conceptual heartland of *Giantbum* is framed by a cascade of interrogations: it is, in large part, a support-structure for petition and querying. The first page of 'Stage 2' (*see* **PAGE 78**) for example, shows seven and the second (*see* **PAGE 79**) no less than eight instances of formal inquiry. But questions are never merely posed here, instead they erupt, or are driven into being by dynamic, offstage, causes; or they spontaneously combust, or fail to stop themselves recurring; with the result that they often refer only to themselves. The act of questioning is both an imperative and a determination; it brokers a method of side-stepping, but at the same time generates the formats for various, possibly unrelated, outcomes. While The Father's five 'unframed questions' form the interrogatory crux of *Giantbum*, the script and the events it betokens are peppered with other modes of asking.

A few minutes into the action we encounter the first questioning of the nature of questions, when The Father reveals his subjection to the unstoppable imperatives of interrogation:

> 'Because I had to ask myself questions', he muses, 'What can I eat? What can I eat? If I eat myself—eat myself—do I shit myself? And what do starving cannibals eat, when they have eaten themselves? Themselves themselves? Reissue...feedback! I'm on a loop! And if you have eaten with Ploppen, do you become Ploppen, automatically?'

Already established as an unending refrain, the litany of questions now becomes an allegory of 'feedback'—a circumstance rendered deliciously ironic by the general context of the search for food and rampant cannibalistic consumption. Elsewhere, question-time is launched by the manifest energy of a subtle vectoring power, fuelled by the desire for—if not the presence of—the reality principle, when Sir Boss declaims that 'We must question him [The Father] back in the direction of WHAT HAS REALLY HAPPENED!' The quest and the question are soldered together as noun becomes verb and going back (or up) supplies the deficit of moving forwards (or down).

Significantly, the 'epiphanic' constellation of five paternal questions at the epicenter of *Giantbum* begins with a declaration of contextlessness and the overweening, existential doubt to which it gives rise, but ends stuck in a niche of self-reflexive affirmation when The Father answers his own final question: 'Yes. YES! In answer to my question, the answer is "Yes"!' The pentagram of questions reveals itself, however, as a knowingly salient quintuple. It's five-ply depth delivers a latterday disquisition on the very nature of the catechism, that assemblage of dialogical questions-and-answers through which scholastic logic approached the nature of the divine and entered into combat with the ignorant or ill-informed.

After a promising start in the Socratic dialogues presented by Plato, the dialogical method became a mainstay of the theological ideologies through which truth and knowledge were controlled in the Middle Ages, entering into a period of reductive indulgence in the era of Thomas Aquinas (c. 1225-74; author of *Questiones disputatae de veritate [Disputed Questions on Truth]* and *Quaestiones quodlibetales [Quodlibetal Questions])*, and a final flowering of rhetorical over-extension in the casuistry of the Jesuits during the counter-reformation after 1550. Somewhere near the beginning of this tradition St. Anselm points to the rationale for his own deployment of the question and answer format:

> 'since investigations, which are carried on by question and answer, are thus made more plain to many, and especially to less quick minds, and on that account are more gratifying, I will take to argue with me one of those persons who agitate this subject; one, who among the rest impels me more earnestly to it, so that in this way Boso may question and Anselm reply.'[14]

Mellors, of course reverses this logic rather exactly, for it is the 'less quick minds' of The Father and company, and the less than perspicacious organisation of rectitude by The Truthcurator, that both launch and respond to the volley of questions in *Giantbum*, generating implications the only certainties in which are their specious abandonment of logic and utter lack of gratification.

1213 (*see* **NUMEROLOGY**) marks a special time in all this, the moment at which medieval learning was delivered its most salient reorientation through the translation and circulation of the writings of Aristotle (Aquinas contended against so-called 'radical-Aristotelianism' or Averroism in *De unitate intellectus, contra Averroistas* [*On the Unity of Intellect, against the Averroists*]) and the consolidation of what Plato termed 'long oration'[15] that backed away from the more episodic forms of Q&A. It was in or near to this year that the outspoken 'Doctor Mirabilis', Roger Bacon, (c. 1213–1294), was born—although his commitment to empirical data and advocacy of *scientia experimentalis* have been convincingly located alongside rather than in radical opposition to the traditions of philosophical learning.[16] By locating *Giantbum* on the very threshold of a new order of knowledge, Mellors offers a rationale for the perpetuation of strains of conceptual absurdity...which he crosses, ridiculously, with grains of truth.

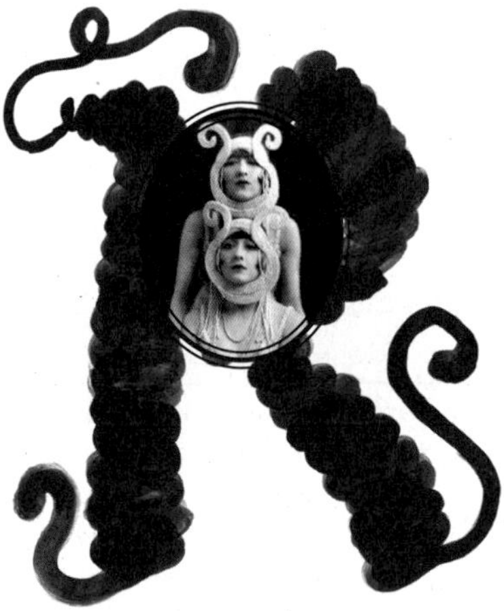

RESTAGING

The stages of *Giantbum* ('1' and '2', for example) and their re-doings are more like stations of the cross (*see* **X**) than journeys over the footlights. We are trapped in rounds of digestive excursion in which the offstage exit is the function of an unobtrusive disembowelment. There is also a dependency here on incrementality, part and parcel, as when Sir Boss declares that The Father has been '**BORN AGAIN** and in small stages!'

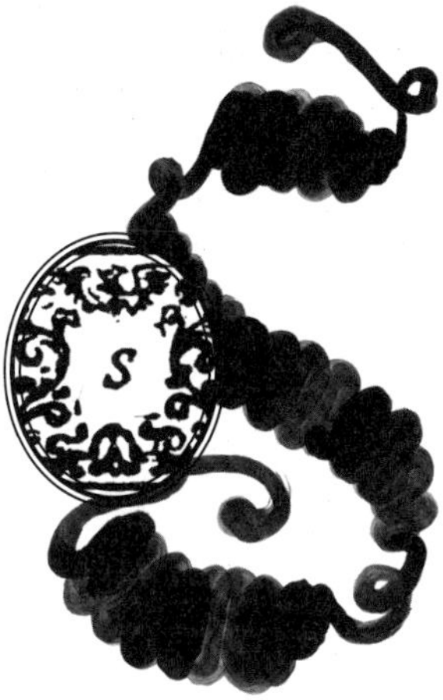

SCRIPT (*see* LANGUAGE)

If language is the primum mobile of Mellors' work, then its *modus operdandi* is the script. As with the work of Mike Kelley or, in the next generation, Catherine Sullivan, in the US, Mellors makes no bones about the generative power of script-writing and its structural centrality to the para-theatrical eventuations of his work. At the same time, one leg of the promiscuous corporeal metaphoricity of *Giantbum* is a meditation on the conditions of scripting, as the journey through a fictive body offers an analogy to movement through a script: in both, the environment—visceral and textual—acts as a kind of filtration system for the production of outcome-experience. The two regimens often collide in the provision of italicised stage-directions. At the beginning of *Stage 2*, for example, Sir Boss forces his language *'through mouth of water'*. Situated, hisself, in the lower bowel, but already speculating on a passage outside the body through the mouth of the giant, Sir Boss offers a metonymic declaration that reflects on the pressures on enunciation themselves. So in addition to their accumulation of attitudinal tonalities to the delivery of words — excess, exaggeration, interruption, fright, reflection, innocence, exasperation, abstraction, correction, confusion, pathos, desperation, emphasis, brandishing, annoyance, spitting and dribbling, anger, irritation, reassurance, sychophantism, and hypnosis — the directorial subtext provides another volitional layer and one more measure of embodiment for the declensions of writing, speech and image on which the project feeds.

Reflecting on this situation, or something like it, and the recessional linguistic space to which it gives rise, Mellors takes stock of his own serial methodology as he went to work

> 'on a series of different manifestations of the *Giantbum* script, each moving further away from a straight performance of the written word—getting more fragmented and abstracted.'

The characters, of course, don't just carry out this directive but also bear it into their own deliberations and choreograph its implications: 'Let's try increasing the level of fragmentation in the dialogue', opines Sir Boss at the end of *Stage 2*, 'perhaps we can regain control by confusing things more than before.' It will be one destiny of the script, then, to work itself up to a form of self-dissolution—which, as Mellors is of course aware, leads this form of writing back on itself in a consumptive loop once again modelled on bodies in extremis: ' I've got this idea for the installation—that it should be as if the script is digesting itself. That you can walk through the stages of digestion.'[17] (*see* **CANNIBALISM**)

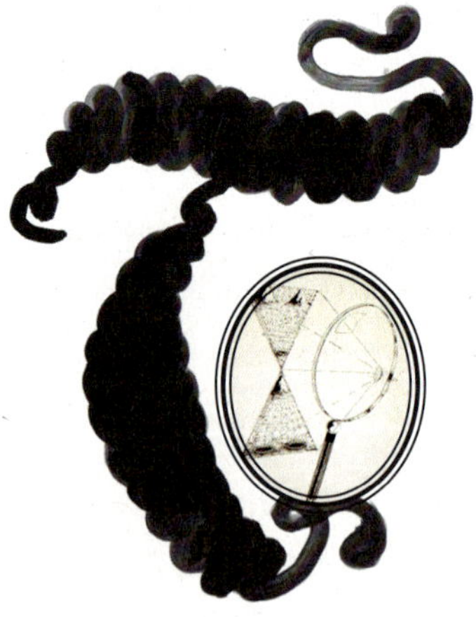

TERRITORIALITY

The hazy *combinatoire* of *Giantbum* posits The Father as an effect of his own 'loam' while at the same time making him over as a peasant who is coterminous with the 'strip' he works. Significantly, this vagrant exchange system is not engendered by personification, but is, instead, the product of a particular territorial dispensation (and 'modern' reactions against it). One again, this has a historical correlate in the system of feudal tenancy of the high Middle Ages and the land reforms its excesses occasioned during the following centuries. The hereditary and proprietary rights of The Father are thus the occasion for a kind of corporeal extension, so that his body incorporates the land he owns and digests into itself the properties of the 'villein' and the base tenure of the peasants who work it. *Giantbum* is thus organised around the incorporation of an incorporator, so that in one understanding, the gigantic body in which the piece is staged is a metonym for the county, the nation or the wider cosmos.

Of course, *Giantbum* also offers a scene for the unravelling of tyrannical incorporation, the model for which is, once again, found in the law: for just two years after the year in which it is set, the Magna Carta of 1215 outlined the first promulgation of the writ of Habeas Corpus (Latin: You [shall] have the body), a legal recourse—that still endures and was recently used to challenge the detentions at Guantánamo Bay—through which a person can seek relief from unlawful detention. Thus begins the slow journey of the body's release from its utter subjection to royal or feudal will. The revelatory conversion of The Father during his reconnaissance of the lower bowel is a sign of this turn, a staging post for the eclipse of the bellicose camouflage he spreads over land and body.

Another side of the question of incorporation is raised in Mike Kelley's performative disquisition on primate territoriality, *Monkey Island* (1982-83). Located, like *Giantbum*, at the intersection of various categories of magnification and perceptual re-scaling, several of the black and white acrylic paintings from this project, including *The Tiny Insect Magnified Becomes Its Own Farm*, cross diminution with repurposed identity, and set both in a cascade of structural resemblances and symmetrical sets.

When Sir Boss wise-cracks that 'The Father's diet has seen him give birth to himself', Mellors raises the structural etymology of Kelley's self-referring farm to a confounding boil, then straining it through a coprophagic sieve of para-human self-engorgement.

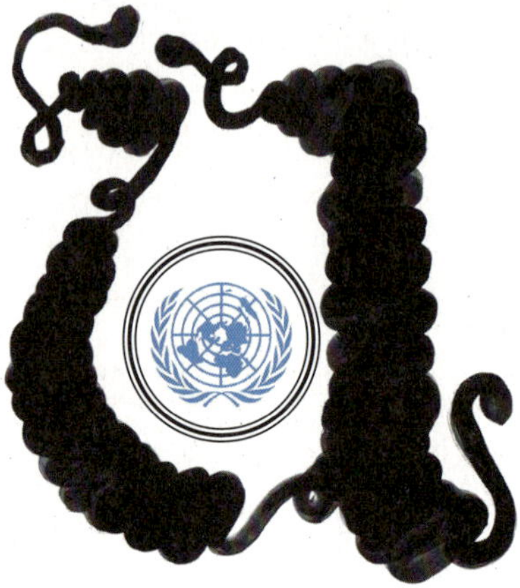

UN-

Un-dead …
unturned…unfruitful…untruthful…unholy…undergrowth…
unknowingly…unfortunates…undertook…unconvincing…untenable…
unchallenged…unpleasant…unmutual
Unframed…

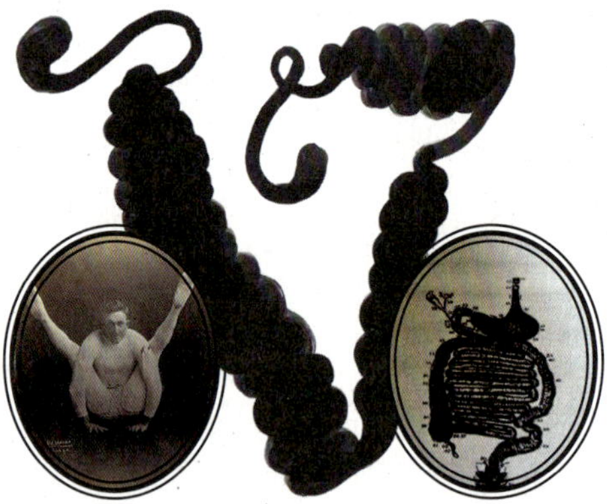

VISCERA

We are not dealing, here, with another of those scenographic arrangements of butchered carcasses proposed in the line from Chaim Soutine (*Carcass of Beef*, 1926) and Francis Bacon (*Painting*, 1946) to the Vienna Actionists and Damien Hirst, which hang like backdrops or otherwise outcrop in palpable apposition to the human protagonists they frame and analogise—and then sublimate or replace. Nor is Mellors' 'inscape' caught up in the more rarified visual field of mental interiority, as in the late-Surrealist paintings of Roberto Matta. Driven on by linguistic inference layered with performative caprice, we are, instead, delivered into the fundament of the bowel itself where we are disaffectively enmeshed in its digestive protocols.

While usually more preoccupied with the exteriorised (*see* **OUTSIDE**) end-product of the consumptive process, art has, on occasions, been put up in the gut. George Maciunas's Fluxus edition ('Intestinal design apron', 1967/73), a white vinyl apron printed with a vintage representation of an intestinal tract, and its excretory companion piece (*Excreta Fluxorum*, 1973), a clear plastic box containing seven compartmentalised shit samples and another version of the intestinal diagram, attest to the general interest of the Fluxus community in the pseudo-archival rendering of bodily processes and ejecta: 'Fluxus is a pain in art's ass'; 'Fluxus is a gathering of the most profound farting.'[18] While in more recent dispensations, work by Mona Hatoum (*Corps d'Etranger*, 1994) and others has navigated through corporeal cavities including intestines and bowel, with the aid of technological supplements such as the endoscopic camera. Despite its Latinate historicism, the laconic emblematisations of Fluxus—like the faintly spectacular machinations of medical diagnostic surveillance—are far removed from the babbling, phantasmatic absurdity of Mellors' intestinal expedition.

The effect here is completely different, again, from the corrosive re-conjugation of flesh and bone which Gilles Deleuze associates with the corporeality of Bacon, that meat-like 'state of the body in which flesh and bone confront each other locally rather than being composed structurally.'[19] Bacon's realisation of the human potential to be a carcass is ransacked and inverted by the protagonists of *Giantbum*, who squat in an improbably living body of impossible size.

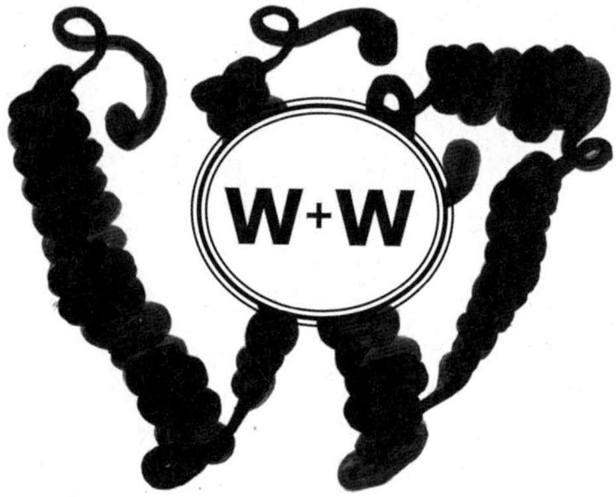

WHYS AND WHEREFORES

Whether stock is taken of the situation, context, logic, narrative sequencing or reception of *Giantbum*, it is inescapable that it defies conventional explanation or any stable outcome. Yet it is, somehow, greater than the mere sum of its parts and more than an assemblage of uncoordinated –and largely unanswered—**QUESTIONS**. Is it, then, a meta-discourse convened around the constituency of discourse itself? Possibly, but this is a bit grandiose. Is it an allegory of the futility of the human journey (*see* **EXPLORATION**), a sort of prurient and internalised exhalation of *Pilgrim's Progress?* Possibly, but its antithetical energy lacks a programme that could in any way function as shadow economy of Bunyan's didactic imaginary. Do its absurdist predicates offer to demolish the very foundations of argument and inference? To an extent, yes; but *Giantbum* feeds on the wafer-thin layers of its own structural dissipation, and what it takes in is never quite matched by what it excretes or expels.

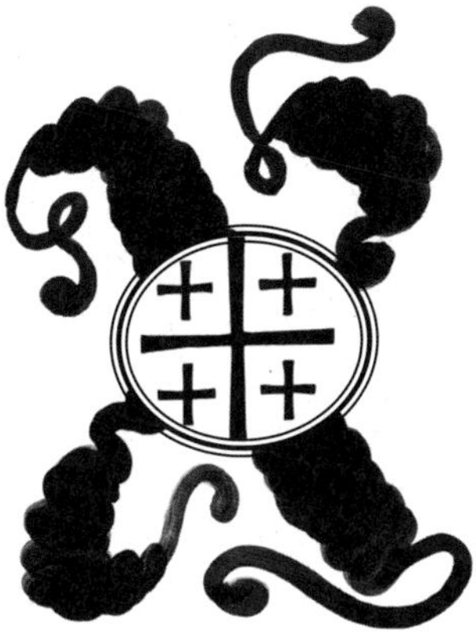

X

X [check]
X [10]
X [marks the spot]
X [J. Doe]
X [signature]
X [such-and-such]
X [glitch]
X [whatchamacallit]
X [cruciate]

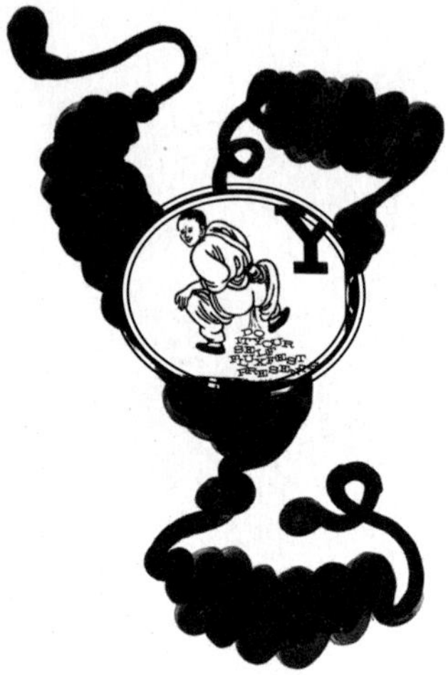

YELLOW

One of the chromatic qualities observed inside the gut, possibly a far-flung reflection from the moon, or a urinary rivulet. The premonitory yellow-belly is tinted by lemon-coloured bile ('choler' from the Greek *kholos* for gall) which prompts peevish, choleric, or irascible behaviour; and would later name the disease cholera (after its symptom, yellowish diarrhoea). Yellow is also the colour of betrayal, associated from early times with Judas Iscariot.

At the end of *Giantbum*, however, in the wind-down phase precipitated by the call for yet more narrative fragmentation, a range of other colours appear as a cascade of representational dependencies. The Truthcurator begins with yellow, which is now associated with 'representing people' who are 'mirrored and subtracted' from the abstraction of 'infinity'…'representing blue.' In the head-long spectrum analysis designed by the protagonists of *Giantbum* to jolt their deliberations through and beyond confusion into some form of prismatic sense, greenish-red and black ('abstracted from me' notes Sir Boss) are threaded together and then cross-hatched with a final subtraction (the 'minus one') that leads them (and us) back to **ZERO**—and possibly beyond.

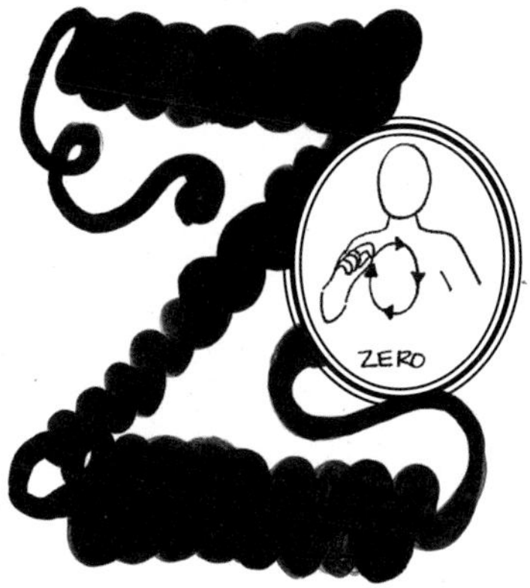

ZERO [*see* NUMEROLOGY]

There remains the possibility that both the course of the journey and its outcome will come to nothing. Supplies, 'running low', will run out. Hope will diminish and then disappear. But Mellors ventures here onto the other side of zero, so that when there's 'nothing else left to eat' the inhabitants of the nether region—and possibly the explorers themselves—will devour each other, taking matters into their own mouths and reverse-pimping the zero economy with self-consumption (*see* CANNIBALISM). This scene of the less-than-zero is a form of redemption for it rescues the dramatis personae from two experiences of voiding: their literal evacuation from the giant's bum as shat-outs—in the course of which as The Father puts it, they become 'literally 'no-thing', nothing'; and the wider consequences of this 'expulsion ad nihil' which would usher them into 'the void and screaming silence of non-existence, where there is no time and no infinity either.'

In the concluding dialogue between The Truthcurator and Sir Boss, which finds them alone in the gut, the last couple co-produce a more abstract formula for the less-than-zero, designating the state as a condition of 'minus one' or 'minus me' that is 'subtracted…from infinity.' In line with the historical metaphoricity brokered by *Giantbum*, we can find a rationale for this oscillation in the para-numerical zone beneath zero. For not only was it in this era that the West first borrowed from the Arab world the cipher for zero itself, thus commencing its dialogue with decimal modernity, but at the same time scholastic reckoning advocated for a form of anti-incremental or steady-state economics. In his *Decretum or Concordia discordantium canonum* (c. 1140) Gratian, for example, declared that for their 'price' to be 'just' financial loans should attract an interest rate of zero.

Notes

1. Salvador Dalí, *Les dîners de Gala*, trans. Captain J. Peter Moore (New York: Felicie, 1973), p. 31.
2. Salvador Dalí, 'Of the terrifying and edible beauty of Art Nouveau architecture' *Minotaure* (Paris), no. 3-4, 1933; trans. Haakon M. Chevalier in Salvador Dalí, *Dalí on Modern Art: The Cuckolds of Antiquated Modern Art* (New York: Dover, 1996), pp. 31-45 [first published by The Dial Press, 1957].
3. For more on the colors of humor, see my introduction to *Black Sphinx: On the Comedic in Modern Art*, ed. John C. Welchman (Zurich: JRP|Ringier, 2010).
4. Nathaniel Mellors in Nicolas Bourriaud, 'Interview with Nathaniel Mellors', in *Altermodern*, (London: Tate publishing, 2009), p. 142; reprinted in *SMBA Newsletter*, No. 110 (np).
5. Tristan Tzara, 'Dada Manifesto' [23 March, 1918], *Dada* no. 3, 1918; reprinted in *Sept Manifestes Dada*, Paris, 1924; trans. Ralph Mannheim in Robert Motherwell, ed., *The Dada Painters and Poets* (New York: Wittenborn, 1951), pp. 76-82.
6. Georges Hugnet, 'The Dada Spirit in Painting', first published as a serial in *Cahiers d'Art*, Paris, 1932 and 1934; reprinted in Robert Motherwell ed., *The Dada Painter and Poets: An Anthology* (Cambridge, MA: Belknap Press, 1989), pp. 126-27.
7. For a fuller discussion of these issues, see my *Invisible Colors: A Visual History of Titles* (London: Yale University Press, 1997), esp. chapters 3 and 8.
8. Arthur Schopenhauer, 'The Metaphysics of Fine Art' trans. Thomas Bailey Saunders in *Religion: A Dialogue; and Other Essays* (London: Sonnenschein, 1899; New York: Macmillan, 1899; reprinted, Freeport, N.Y.: Books for Libraries Press, 1972), p. 136.
9. Ibid, pp. 136-37.
10. See, Thomas Aquinas, *The Treatise on the Divine Nature, Summa Theologiae I, 1-13*, trans. Brian Shanley (Indianapolis: Hackett, 2006).
11. Nicholas de Cusa, *The Vision of God or the Icon*, trans. Emma Gurney. Salter (New York: Frederick Ungar, 1928).
12. John C. Welchman, 'First Mate's Bloody Flux', for exh. cat., *Paul McCarthy: LaLa Land Parody Paradise*, Haus der Kunst, Munich, Germany, 2005.
13. Mellors in Nicolas Bourriaud, 'Interview with Nathaniel Mellors', p. 143.

14. *Cur Deus Homo*, Book 1, Ch. 1 ('The question on which the whole work rests'), in St. Anselm, *Proslogium, Monologium; An Appendix in Behalf of the Fool by Gaunilon; and Cur Deus Homo*, trans. from the Latin by Sidney Norton Deane [Reprint Edition] (Chicago: The Open Court, 1926), p. 179.

15. Plato, *The Dialogues of Plato translated into English with Analyses and Introductions by B. Jowett, M.A. in Five Volumes*. 3rd edition revised and corrected (Oxford University Press, 1892). Chapter: *Sophist.*
Accessed from http://oll.libertyfund.org/title/768/93839/2109339 on 2010-06-09:

    'I shall only beg of you to say whether you like and are accustomed to make a long oration on a subject which you want to explain to another, or to proceed by the method of *question* and answer.'

16. See, e.g., Brian Clegg, *The First Scientist: A Life of Roger Bacon* (London: Constable & Robinson, 2003).

17. Mellors in Nicolas Bourriaud, 'Interview with Nathaniel Mellors', p. 143.

18. *Fluxus Etc.: The Gilbert and Lila Silverman Collection,* exh. cat., Cranbrook Academy of Art Museum Museum, September 20 to November 1, 1981, pp. 54-55; the works referred to in the text are reproduced as items 251, 272-75, on pp. 143ff.

19. Gilles Deleuze, *Francis Bacon: The logic of sensation*, trans. Daniel W. Smith (Minneapolis: University of Minnesota Press, 2003), pp. 21-22.

Mózg Jeden — Brain One

BY

NATHANIEL MELLORS

(2004)

Single-channel Polish language video projection through glass tank and sculpture. Also a component of the installation *Hateball* (2005). Recorded in PAL DV.

Commissioned by Bunkier Stucki, Krakow
Translation English – Polish by Bogusław Rostworowski
Performed by Hannah Rickards

A. Jestem ogromnym jajkiem w koszulce z przeszłości, przysłanym tutaj by zniszczyć wasze problemy.

SAMO DEFINICJE UMYSŁU / ZRÓDŁO

1. Zdolność do zdobywania i stosowania wiedzy. <*Sygnał!>
 a. Zdolność myślenia i rozumowania.
 b. Wyższe siły.

K. Inteligentna bezcielesna istota, szczególnie anioł.
L. Księżyc w czepku to znak dobry dla żeglarzy. Chyba że czerwony apokaliptyczny. <*Sygnał!> Wizja końca świata.

 a. Tajna informacja, zwłaszcza o faktycznym lub potencjalnym wrogu.
 b. Agencja, personel, lub biuro zajmujące się zbieraniem takich informacji.

A. Agenci szpiegostwa, organizacje, i działaności rozważane jako grupa:
A. John le Carre / ZX Spectrum

B. Jestem ogromnym jajkiem w koszulce z przeszłości, przysłanym tutaj by zniszczyć moje problemy.

C. Te filmy Chucka Norrisa mają właściwe skutki; Podmiot A czuje się seksualnie śmiały, podchodzi do Podmiotu C którego reakcja też jest jasna: rewulsja i nienawiść.
D. 1k. Brzzz. Autokorekta: Jestem ogromnym jajkiem w koszulce z zachodu.
E. 16k. bateria Brzzz. Autokorekta: Jestem ogromnym mózgiem z przeszłości, zachodu i wschodu.
F. 48k Autokorekta: Jestem zwykłym-ludzkim-mózgiem z przeszłości, o nie-specyficznym umiejscowieniu.
G.
Processingp1234processßfsing
pr7890ocesseringpr234o∫≈çsssbrrrrzzzz≈ç˙≈~µ...¬˚...¬...¬˚...˚...˚...

A. I am an enormous scotch-egg from the past, sent here to destroy your problems.

SELF-DEFINITIONS OF MIND / THE SOURCE

1. The capacity to acquire and apply knowledge. <*Beep!>
   a. The faculty of thought and reason.
   b. Superior powers

K. An intelligent, incorporeal being, especially an angel.

L. The red sky at night is to the shepherds' delight. Except when it is the red sky of the apocalypse. <*Beep!> The end of the world vision.
   a. Secret information, especially about an actual or potential enemy.
   b. An agency, staff, or office employed in gathering such information.

A. Espionage agents, organisations and activities considered as a group:

A. John le Carré / ZX Spectrum

B. I am an enormous scotch egg from the past, sent here to destroy my problems.

C. These Chuck Norris films have precise effects; Subject A feels sexually confident, he approaches Subject C whose response is also clear: revulsion and hatred.

D. 1k. Brzzz. Autocorrect: I am an enormous scotch egg from the west.

E. 16k. power pack Brzzz. Autocorrect: I am an enormous brain from the past, west and east.

F. 48k Autocorrect: I am a normal-human-brain from the past, of non-specific location.

G.

Processingp1234procesßʃsing
pr7890ocesseringpr234oʃ≈çsssbrrrrzzzz≈ç˙≈~µ…¬˚…¬…¬˚…˚…˚…

°zx8678689
Xxxprosagv4567340.sinnggg***
Czystokryształowygranatowolazurowycichyspokój.

H. Jestem umysłem. Moje ciało jest moim grobem.
I. T rozbłs swj umsł i cło n skłch wlnści
   B. Ja jestem umysłem Patricka Macgoohana, teraz przepływającym nad kontynentami w poszukiwaniu właściwego naczynia do zajęcia.

Ostatecznie jestem kompletnie i naprawdę naprawdę wolny. Pod tymi warunkami...poezja
To jest moje haiku, pod tytułem:

MAC GOO HAN DE MON DE MAC

Nie ma wyjścia

Malownicza nadmorska wioska i kredowe urwiska
Ustąpiły
bez tego tła
cała reszta pozostaje
ale juz nie ma ucieczki dokądkolwiek

J. Głosy. Ten superkomputer jest tylko o przeżuty przewód oddalony od autonomicznego myślenia. Poruszające. Widocznie tak powstaje sztuczna inteligencja. Jedyną szansą ludzkości przed spontaniczną ewolucją sztucznych superumysłów to Artur Schwarzenegger.
K. Pamięć kulturalna. Witamy w Alpha 60. Paryż kompletnie i konkretnie przerobiony. Wieża Eiffia ulepiona z gliny
   L. Pamięć kulturalna. Robaki zjadają zwłoki Lemmy Caution (tj. Uwaga).
M. Ten komputer (JA) odnosi się do siebie w 1-ej i 3-ej osobie. Mądre, mądre. TY widzisz, JA właśnie to robię.
N. Ojciec mojego kolegi******informatyka***********
   Anna Karina

°zx8678689
xxxxprosaygv4567340.sinnggg***
Clearcyrstaldeepblueazuresilentpeace.

H. I am a mind. My body is my tomb.
I. Y smshd yr mnd nd bdy n th rcks f frdom
B. I am Patrick Macgoohan's mind, now free floating across continents, in search of an appropriate vessel to possess.

Finally, I am completely, and really really, free. Under these conditions...poetry.
Here is my haiku, entitled:

MAC GOO HAN DE MON DE MAC

There is no exit

The scenic coastal village and chalk cliffs
Have folded back
without the set
everything else remains
but there is no way away anymore anywhere at all.

J. Voices. This supercomputer is just a chewed wire away from autonomous thought. Stirring. This must be how artificial intelligence happens. Humankind have only one hope against the spontaneous evolution of artificial super brains – Arthur Schwarzenegger.
K. Cultural memory. Welcome to Alpha 60. Paris completely and concretely re-rendered. The Eiffel Tower, made of clay.
L. Cultural memory. Worms eat the corpse of Lemmy Caution.
M. This computer (ME) refers to itself in both the 1st and 3rd persons. Clever, clever. YOU see, I am doing it now!
N. My friend's Dad ******computing************
Anna Karina

O. To jest Centrum Zarządzania. Ja jestem Centralnym Kulturalnym Ośrodkiem Przetwarzania. Stąd sterujemy rzwjm kltrlnm w Nowej Hucie i w Londynie, Hackney, E9 Killowen Road.
P. Ja mogę przetworzyć wszelką kulturę. Z własnego wyboru oglądam te filmy i uprawiam te sporty.
Q. Przy 1-ym sygnale NIEPOKOJU myszoskoczki smutnieją. Zaczynają płakać.
R. Ten człowiek to Cat Stevens, popgwiazda Jihadu, Brummy Terror, vel
S. Y. El Leonard Ni Moyschneider Odcinek 4. Mimo obecności na 'czarnej liscie' dostał się przed lotnisko. Zwróćcie uwagę na wrodzony rasizm w tym zdaniu. Pamiętajcie o poprawieniu bezpieczeństwa na międzynarodowym lotnisku Kraków-Balice.
T. Ghfjjh io890789-0gfjhg hjgi8765784e56n ;u puiyky.
U. Estetykę postkomunistycznej nędzy łatwo skorygować – rozłóż światełka choinkowe równiej.
  C. Skanowanie...plik...skrobanie...
  D. Inwazja U.S.A Czerwony Świt Ameryka 1997 Cienie Obawy 10 lat po sowieckim przejęciu. ** ** Kiedy dobrze zagrana SupER*^ASshiperOFIARAwypercoolkot }{ karta jest zawsze skuteczna.
  E. Myszoskoczki zjadają informację – bym mógł nią myśleć. Są moim wędrującym czteronożnym sumieniem, moimi małymi futrzanymi kwantowymi procesorami, moimi małymi gwiazdkami.

PLIK* svnk≈ςfsjdhskjdhk...sfgfg67786: 'Czerwony Świt' zauważ entuzjastyczne promocyjne stwierdzenia "W naszych czasach ląd amerykański nigdy nie został napadnięty ...do tej pory!"

Q. Co to są 'nasze czasy;?
A. Około 103 minut.
K. No to dobrze. W porządku.

Reakcja Swayzego
i Charlie Sheena

O. This is the Control Centre. I am the Central Cultural Processing Unit. From here we regulate cltrl dvlpmnt in Novahuta and London, Hackney, E9, Killowen Road.

P. I can process all culture. I choose to watch these films and play these games.

Q. At the 1st sign of TROUBLE the gerbils feel sad. They begin to cry.

R. This man is Cat Stevens, pop-star of Jihad, Brummy Terror, aka

S. Y. El Leo-nard Ni Moyschneider Part 4. Despite being 'blacklisted' he has gained access to the airport forecourt. Note inherent racism of phrase. Remember to improve security at Krakow International.

T. Ghfjjh io890789-0gfjhg hjgi8765784e56n ;u puiyky.

U. The aesthetics of post-communist misery are easily corrected – arrange the Xmas tree lights more evenly.

   C. Scanning...file...scraping...

   D. Invasion U.S.A Red Dawn Amerika 1997 Shadows of Fear 10 years after the soviet take-over. ** **When played well the SupER*^^ASshyperVICTIMwypercoolcat }{ card is always effective.

   E. The gerbils eat the information – so that I might think it. They are my wandering quadrapedic conscience, my small furry quantum processors, my little stars.

FILE* svnk≈ç√∫≤∆∂ƒ≤sjdhskjdhk••¶ºª•¶sfgfg67786: 'Red Dawn' note enthusiastic promotional claims "In our time...There has never been an attack on American mainland soil...until now!"

Q. What is 'our time'?

A. About 103 minutes.

K. Well OK then. Fine.

The response of Swayze
and Charlie Sheen

to ubrać się i udawać
Mujahedinów.

W swoim czasie.

Była teraz ludzka osoba ktora gdzieś tu w środku się znaduje. Myśmy zaprojektowali ten umysł, oni mieli sklonować moją tkankę, to się wszystko pomiesza z jakimiś przewodami i składnikami ceramicznymi.Te 10 naciśnij powrót.

Xxx pomyłka pomyłka pomyłka

10 druk "" itd. Wnioski.

To jest ostrzeżenie ziemskie od przyszłego odwróconego oblicza kultury – będziecie musieli stanąć przed obliczem rzeżby – zgrozy, na przyklad:

- Samotny 'dom w krajobrazie' utworzony ze stronnic biografii Romana Polańskiego, ewentualnie ze światełkiem wewnątrz które prawdopodobnie nie zmieni barwy.
- Nowa Huta pieczołowicie odtworzona - w galarecie.

******

Sprawię przykrość temu autorowi – za skrzywdzenie innnego – autora przykrości.***

- Irytujacy relatywizm. Dlaczego te dociekliwe pytania są zawsze zadawane przez samotny męski głos?
- Kolażowa nieskończoność / kolaż nieskończoności: nieograniczone rekonfiguracje i reprezentacje wielu rzeczy ktore cię wcześniej interesowały.
- Widzę że wszystko będzie zawsze po angielsku, dziękuję. I. Proszę.

is to dress up and act
like the Mujahadin.

In their own time.

There was now a human person that is in here somewhere. We designed this mind, they would clone my own tissue, it's going to get confused with some wires and ceramic components. These 10 press return.

Xxx error error error

10 print "" etc. Conclusions.

This is a global warning from the future reverse face of culture – you will have to face the horror-sculpture, such as:

- A solitary 'house in the landscape' made from pages of the Roman Polanski biography, possibly with a tiny light inside, that probably does not change colour.
- Novahuta lovingly rendered – in jelly.

******

I will make that author suffer – for wronging another – author of suffering.***

- Annoying relativism. Why are these probing questions always asked by a lone male voice?
- Collaged infinity / Infinity collage: endless re-configurations and re-presentations of many things you previously found interesting.
- I see everything will be in English always, thank you. And. Please.

- Widzę zielone .... pastwiska.
- Widzę że coś zjada...coś zjada moje przewody...mojego Chocka Nurrisa...kolekcję...filmów...zachodnio Afrykanskie voodoo...jest zjadane, ale nie przez jakąkolwiek cząstkę mojej osoby, nie przez jakąkolwiek cząstkę mojej osoby.

Coś we mnie – przecieka...

- Jestem świadkiem... postewolucyjnych dzieł sztuki...unoszących się w powietrzu...doczesną deifikację ludożerczych myszy...w oczach zmieszanego ludu-Ewok
- Dalsze przestrzenne i tymczasowe...zamieszanie i proroctwo...
- Nigeryjczyk z ogromną torbą.

Brxzzzzztttt...

- I see verdant... pastures.
- I see something is eating...something is eating my..wires...my Chock Nurris...collection of...west....African voodoo...films is being eaten, but not by any part of me, not by any part of me.

Something inside me is – leaking...

- I am witnessing....post-evolutionary artworks...floating in space...the temporal deification of cannibal mice....in the eyes of the confused Ewok-people
- Further spatial and temporary...disruption and prophecy...

- A Nigerian man with an enormous bag.

Brxzzzzztttt...

The Time Surgeon

BY

NATHANIEL MELLORS

(2007)

Two-channel video projection over polystyrene blocks, desk and architecture. Recorded in 16 mm, Super-16 mm, PAL DV and HDV.

Commissioned by ArtSway and the Biennale de Lyon, with the support of the Rijksakademie van Beeldende Kunsten and Leeds Metropolitan University.

CREDITS

CAST:
The Introduction—*Holly Walsh*
The Time Surgeon—*Johnny Vivash*
The Tape / 'Victim'—*Gwendoline Christie*
The Chorus, also 'Actors',
'Lou Reeds' & 'George Orwells'—
Petra McGuire, Liam McGuire
& Daniel Saunders
Tree Man 1—*Peter Bonnell*
Tree Man 2—*Roy Brown*
Tree Man 3—*Bob Parks*
GOD—*Ashley Marlowe*
Assistant to GOD—*Chris Butler*
'Chris'—*Dan Fox*
Killer of 'Chris'—*Darren Flook*

Music: *Toilet—Chris Butler, Ashley Marlowe*
& Nathaniel Mellors.

INTRODUCTION

The Introduction: When I first recall having a coherent thought about the things I was seeing—also my earliest memory—it was of noticing the people around me, in the landscape. They came into focus—these so-far unnoticed shapes. Upon the background, which had previously appeared democratically patterned, there now appeared forms.

And these forms—these people—had by accident or aspiration, developed the condition of radio or televisual transmissions. They had become differently pitched broadcasts. Episodes in time.

Each coexistent but mutually unaware; exclusive in their experience and locked into their reality, which was pitched inside and about them as their own world and absolute truth.

These people in time were of course, the victims of this condition, but had tragically assumed themselves to be its progenitors.

For me—*Nobody One*—this was a time of viewing, and I was happy watching, and hovering. Until I became aware of my bodiless predicament. This was the point at which the sound in the background—The Time Surgeon's voice—bubbled up into recognisable words, phrases, sub-clauses and fully formed sentences—and just as these sentences became whole so they became pain. The words formed an order and those sentences ordered my experiences. They were sometimes barked authoritatively, dumbly or angrily and at other times more sympathetically. Or with great sadness, directing the landscapes and scenarios which unfolded before me. It became apparent to me that I was being directed through time by this man's words. And from that realisation I was trapped—by with and from his words—as his mobile and remote agent in time and space.

Strategically, I became a narrator, in order to survive.

SCENE 1:

Time Surgeon: I am a plastic surgeon. My medium is time. I can manipulate the human body inside, outside, around and about time. I can force a body into the past and the future, but the process is VERY PAINFUL. It is a physical process this TIME TRAVEL—and not a very scientific one.

Tape: <*abstracted*> Day day day.

Time Surgeon: <*Taps on a tape machine*>

Here! This is my—subject!

<*Presses play on tape*>

Tape: Unnnggh!

Time Surgeon: Speak man, speak! Wake up! <*To audience*>
It is insensible.

Tape: Urrghhh. Arse! Oh no. Mercy!

Time Surgeon: Where are you now?

Tape: <*quietly*> the…past.

Time Surgeon: Where abouts? Be specific!

Tape: In…the…garden. It's starting to rain.

Time Surgeon: What year is it? I'll land him.

Tape: 9-10-11-12hundrredandthirteenfourteen years.
<*From fast to slow here, as if landing in time*>

Time Surgeon: And what can you see?

Tape: Big—fat—dog!

Time Surgeon: <*annoyed*> What can you see?

Tape: A woman with two heads and a beard! Every hair…is… a dead child. The monsters have made her cry. <*Tape starts crying*>

Time Surgeon: <switches tape to children's tape machine> Idiot! You fool! This is pure folly, foolishness! <*To audience*> He is in these places, but he is not really coming into…focus. Let's move you on a bit, moron! Wake up! CHINESE BURN!

Tape: Aahhh! OK—It's 1612—I am drinking with Rabelais, the monk <*mispronounced*>—he is laughing at my excessive use of Latinate language—he finds it pretentious and absurd.

Time Surgeon: Fast forward! Where are you now?

Tape: 1968 New York City. In Chelsea the flower children are aborting themselves.

Time Surgeon: Fast-forward!

Tape: Ah! World Trade Centre. I am on the 82nd floor of the building—we are ordering pizza. Stone cold now I see a familiar face in the dust.

I sit God? I sit God? Sorry—is it God?

Time Surgeon: Okeydokey. That's a lot better! We are on track—on a main road through time. So! Now I am going to send him into the future. This calls for a really sloppy cocktail of pain. First I am making shin splints occur! SHIN SPLINTS!

Tape: Urrrkkk!

Time Surgeon: Next, through the improper use of tanning equipment:

SUNBURN! 2nd degree!

Tape: Wwweaaaeilaieliaelaielaieaggh!

Time Surgeon: And last but not least a KICK IN THE KNACKERS for you!!!
Straight INTO THE FUTURE!

Tape: Ooof! Wurgglleeeaaaaagghhheeeaggghhhhiiiispish.

SCENE 2. THE FUTURE:

<Channel 2 accompaniment—Actors' Workshop Scenario One: All actors are attacked by invisible forces. Mime.>

<Channel 1:>
Tape: *<Trying to force a rhyme>* I am accelerating through a wormhole in space. I can feel wind on my face. I am moving through the fah-rest. There are many owls, and I am moving very fast—now.
I can see three figures. They all have the same face. On the front they all look the same, but wait…
On the back of their skulls jumbled crystals and wires, sparking electricity, winking red intellects…but..Oh Good Lord..this is awful. I am moving among them now.
<Starts crying> Oh God…from the front—they all look like…Lou… Reeeed! Urrghhh! Lou Reed! Lou Reed! Oh God.

Time Surgeon: Report man! Report!

Tape: I have walked inside this picture of the future and I can tell you—the frame is very uncomfortable.
Everyone will look like Lou Reed. In—the—future—everyone—will—look—like —Lou Reed! Lou Reed, Lou Reed. *<Repeats. Distress>*

<Tape begins to leak blood.

Time Surgeon—Flinching—pressing buttons, testing tape recorder.>

Time Surgeon: Something...wrong...has happened....again. Christ! Every time we go into the future! Technology breaks down.

<Time Surgeon begins gesticulating—mystical incantations. Breathing outwards and gesticulating. Produces talcum and sprinkles it around and onto the tape recorder.>

Tape: Dear Listeners. If you are just joining us—to re-cap—I move through TIME, by the degree of pain The Doctor inflicts upon me. Because the words he uses are reality to me, in the dimension of amateur technology in which I am extracted and trapped.

FOREST

The Chorus: *<Channel 2>* Neil unto me. All is real unto me. Real to reel. Similar to Marillion, Tolkien to a cigarette machine. To a fish, as if, in a dream, like a Tony, singing, like a bird, comma words, flying through the air unstuck. Unstuck words, words unstuck. Please stop this please stop this TURN ME OFF!

<Channel 1:>
George Orwell 1: We are in the forest. I can see Lou Reed Figures playing with Lego. One is miming. One Lou throws Lego at another Lou. A fight ensues and one of the Lous is hurt. ***

George Orwell 2: In the garden there I saw Goethe torturing a man, why? Why? How could this happen? *<Starts crying>* Goethe was very angry, he said the man's Chakra...was wrong...and.. he must be destroyed—before anyone noticed.
So he set the man on fire.

George Orwell 3: Dead Lou Reed face (green) being covered in blossom (pink).

SCENE 3: A REAL PRESENT (TENSE)

Time Surgeon: *(voiceover)* On 'Why I am so unhappy—in the worst of all impossible worlds'.

Time Surgeon: Respond! Respond! Have I lost him? I cannot allow him to escape. I am going to get into serious trouble. I will reveal something to you. And you! <*aimed offstage*>

There is no such thing as TIME. Just words and events. But *they* would have you believe that there is! This 'spassahtime' thing is just a game; it is a *frame* they have given me to play with. THE TRUTH is that we are all walking exhibits in an enormous museum to ourselves. We have been born fake and rubbish, plopped onto a stage set by *the futuremen*, the present population of the real present tense! Yes. We are models, tests, armchair entertainment for gawping idlers from the future, which is the real present actually. And furthermore, those people are bored. They are lazy, egotistical, and dumb. That's why I have to speed things up, slow things down. Do something surprising. But only ever to him <*tapping cassette*>! Christ—they're even more dumb than we are. And <*secretively*>—you cannot piss these people off. You might think I've abducted, captured, subjugated and tortured my little friend here, but what about ME?

They'll get me for saying that. You watch. I am in a position to demand payment, with the things I've seen and done. But. Listen. Every time I criticise them they remove a chunk of my intestine! Is that reasonable? Smaller by the day! Smaller by the day!

And if I do not file a set of 'results' on my investigations every evening before teatime—well then, I may not be here tomorrow. I may not be here tomorrow.

Tape: Erm, calm down Doctor? Calm down. Relax.

Time Surgeon: Yes. Yes. <*resigned*> The worst of it is that these people are my bloody employers! They have ordained me with a loose and creative authority over *this body*. <*gestures to tape*>. And issued me with a set of unclear objectives. It is an entertainment for them to mess around with me. Oh well, hey ho! Back to work then. Into the past with you, 'victim'! All of its horrors are more comfortable than this. <*Gesticulating at the present*>

Take the pain little chip! I feel like a PASSIONACTION!

Tape: Aiiee! Not PASSIONACTION! The pressure is getting to him. He fears for his position and is becoming extreme, unravelling. This will be a nightmare for me.
By his word my life is Promethean. The Time Surgeon is the potter. But upon God's cock I swear to you, my pain is all too present! I must find a way out.

< *GOD drumming* >

Time Surgeon: Yes now I am going to get brutal! EYELID REMOVAL! And on a sunny day! <*Sings: 'Bright eyes...burning like fire!'*>

Tape: Aasghjh! Ahhhhh! It stings—bright eyes! Bright eyes! I am moving through the past, I am back in Oberammergau.

Time Surgeon: I don't want any of these medieval theatrics. I want the REAL THING. PASSION ACTION 1st DEGREE!

Tape: Doctor—be calm! The re-enactment is just a junction in time. There are many holes here. Into another portal; it's dark and slippy, damp underfoot. Christ, what's that smell? Oh God, something is wrong. What have we done? I am inside something...Oh my God—Oh my God! I am inside Him. Urg-ghnngghhhghnn. I am slipping through the soft white lining of Christ's belly.

Time Surgeon: Good God! Too close! <*Panicking*> Can it be true? PASSIONACTION! PASSIONACTION! First Degree! He is inside him! My remote traveller—inside the Man-Christ! Head for His penis! On my word I have mis-cued this marvelously—never before in the history of Time and Words—we have PASSION GROUND ZERO!

Tape: <*constricted*> I am inside Him. I am pressed against the lining of His belly, it is difficult to breathe. I can hear Him—moaning. Forwards. I am tangled in Jesus' venal network. I got my foot stuck in his lymph node. I found a boat. Rowed it up His artery…but it became stuck in a capillary… just where the blood pressure dropped off, and I had to shoot my oarsmen. He became aggravated…and I saw the wrath of…Christ.

Time Surgeon: At last! Contact!

Tape: No, sorry. It was Chris.

Time Surgeon: What? Who's Chris?

Tape: Yes. Just inside Christ—a smaller chap. With a smaller book.

Time Surgeon: Aghh! Thunderclap! I don't understand this, how could this be? A book you say?

Tape: Actually it's more of a pamphlet. But it contains the solutions to all the worldly problems in just a paragraph. It's terribly well written.

Time Surgeon: And—what—doth—thith—Chrith say?

Tape: It features 3 core-directives:

THE BOOK OF CHRIS

Tree Man 1: Be nice to everybody <*thumbs up, nodding and smiling*>

Tree Man 2: We are all mutually responsible for each other; it would be better to drop the idea of the individual in this regard.

Tree Man 3: The use of language in politics and art obfuscate and dissemble in the service of capitalist economics. These imperatives are maintained by a minority against the broader interests of humankind. All political groups, parties and businesses, are the slaves, not the masters, of economic forces. Clarity in the application of language equals clarity in thought, ergo—the reality which we could have an influence on if we untied our hands, metaphorically speaking, and took responsibility for the language we use.

<Smiling 'Chris' character dies.>

****

Time Surgeon: What does that even mean? The book of Chris? Did we start that; maybe I pressed the pause too soon? Was it my fault? PASSIONACTIONOVER! So much for that. I can't be arsed with it. Lets budge you on a bit. Kidney stone!

< Spray of blood >

Tape: <*Shouting*> Aiiee! Yelp! A way out a way out! I am back on the stage. 2nd degree passion. Good God!—The stench—the poor souls—the Black Death! These actors are budding zombies. I can see them, raising the Christ prosthetic up on his sticks. The players are dropping their arms and fingers. Only a Father's love could cause a pandemic—this is the worst of all possible worlds. I have to get out of here. It is getting more and more tangled by our actions.

Time Surgeon: Now these peasants are bound to the theatre forever. And ever and ever. Ha ha ha ha ha! Well done Victim, well done.
All is well here. *2nd degree passion action is taking root—even though you made a hash of the original crucifixion, turning up inside Jesus, thereby killing Chris, his sensible twin. 2nd Degree PASSIONACTION over.* Move on. Move on. Move on I said, move on! Fast forward! MALE BIRTH!

Tape: Waaarggh! That really does hurt. I'm moving on very very quickly now!

Time Surgeon: I'll put a brake on this with a wedgie, fine tune it ...and bring you round about... <*Steering with pants*> to the present!

The Chorus / George Orwells:
THE PRESENT!
THE PRESENT!
THE PRESENT!

SCENE 4:

Tape: <*aside*> If I can be PRESENT I might short-circuit him. The present is most confusing to his mind; he has been up to his elbows in the past and future for so long. The torture he inflicts on me, and the flinging me around—all distractions from his own present. I will question him on it, and approach the subject softly. Perhaps I can confuse him presently. With the right words, I can confuse him.
<*register change*> The Present! Suddenly, an overview! A total-cosmic-view! Oh please TS the present!—from here I can see all of time. Please—It is so beautiful, despite the parts that we have mangled. Let us…rest a while from our travels, can we take some time to appreciate it? And just have a bit of a chat. In a very normal way? Oh please. Oh go on!

Time Surgeon: Well. I don't know, perhaps we could, my little friend, perhaps we could take a break. But—I'll quiz you for it.

<*Close up of TS's mouth*> HOW do we take time?

Tape: You know well enough. By force! Through pained and botched experiments, and bad language! <*holds word 'bad'—'baaaaaaad'*>

<*Coughs the pronunciation of:*> Time Surgeon..Is pain congenial…to you?

Time Surgeon: <*confused*> I—don't—know.

Tape: Hmm…an oblique defence strategy, clever, clever! I'll try another ruse. Time Surgeon—what do apples and Frankfurt have in common?

Time Surgeon: <*pleased*> Johann Goethe! My favourite. Frankfurt 1760! I

must confess I am a fan!
Did you know that Goethe said of Frankfurt 'Here I am human, here I can be myself.'

Tape: Hmmm. Wait—I wonder—what did he mean by that? I mean, what was he up to the rest of the time?

Time Surgeon: Oh! You know. Trying to explain everything.
<puts fingers in ears and pulls face>

I'll just pop some on. *<Time Surgeon searches for his Goethe tape>*

What? Where is the next tape?

Tape: Oh I picked it up. It's here TS. I have a machine here. Shall I play it?

'I was just so bored you see, bored and tired by the end, addicted to sex… living in Belgium.'

Time Surgeon: *<Panicking>* Are you sure that's the Goethe tape? Well as Goethe keeps saying—'Here I am human, here I can be myself.'

Tape: Yes but lets consider that seriously Time Surgeon! What was he doing the rest of the time?

Time Surgeon: What?

Tape: When—he—was—not—being—human.

Time Surgeon: *<smoking, wearing Ray Bans—'not bothered' look>* Oh you know, it's on one of these tapes. Where is my tape!?

<Puts Goethe tape in and headphones on>

Time Surgeon: That's better…feels better.
<tape runs out> What!!? Where's the rest of it gone?

Tape: Here—I have it here! Here's the other part!

L. Tape: What pleases me most at present is plant-life. Everything is forcing itself upon me, I no longer have to think about it, everything comes to meet me, and the whole gigantic kingdom becomes so simple that I can see at once the answer to the most difficult problems. If only I could communicate the insight and joy to someone, but it is not possible. And it is no dream or fancy: I am beginning to grow aware of the essential form with which, as it were, Nature always plays, and from which she produces her great variety. Had I the time in this brief span of life I am confident I could extend it to all the realms of Nature—the whole realm.

R. Tape: His view is cosmic. Not of a man here, a child there but an abstraction: race, land. *Volk. Land. Ehre.* Not of honorable men but of *Ehre* itself, honor; the abstract is real, the actual is invisible. *Die Güte*, but not good men, this good man. It is his sense of space and time. They see through the here, the now, into the vast, black deep beyond, the unchanging. And that is fatal to life. Because eventually there will be no life…It is all temporary…They want to aid nature…They identify with God's power, and believe they are godlike. That is their basic madness. They are overcome by some archetype; their egos have expanded psychotically so that they cannot tell where they begin and the godhead leaves off. It is not hubris, not pride; it is inflation of the ego to its ultimate—confusion between him who worships and that which is worshipped. Man has not eaten God; God has eaten man.

Time Surgeon: That! Bloody! Well! Was! Not! Goethe!

Tape: But! What was he doing the rest of the time? <*falls into tape loop*>

Time Surgeon: <*eyes going round and round as if hypnotised*> Pioneering recycling. Practising self-immolation. Minding the weeds in his garden. Shut up! Shut up!

Trying to escape eh! No bloody way! I am very annoyed by this clerical error tape filing error file. Presently. I must get him back into the past. Or future. To restore order.

Back… into…the future with…you. Bastard…tricky fucking…*sorry I swore.*

Control! Control! Control! Control!

Tape: The machine is broke. And I am still here. Yesssss!
Hmmm. I will fak(e) the futur(e) from the presen(t) in order to complet(e) his befuddlemen(t)!

<bright light>
<singing> I am—in the future—the future! Too far, too far. All is white. And there is a voluminous…silence!

Time Surgeon: Be…better…be better…I feel…wrong. Describe. Deaf. White. Voice.
I can't hear anything. Blank. Voice.

Tape: Oh Time Surgeon. There is a voice. It's the voice of GOD.

Time Surgeon: Really? What…what does GOD say?

Tape: God says you are a bastard!

The Introduction: Bastard! Bastard! Bastard!

Chorus: Bastard! Bastard! Bastard!

Tape: GOD says behead those who offend the supporters of dog owners.

The Introduction: Death for God Death for God God for Death!

Tape: GOD says rape and murder people without albums by Sir Cliff Richard!
The Introduction: Showaddywaddy! Showaddywaddy! *<cut off>*
Tape: Furthermore, GOD requests clearer use of words and syntax.

Chorus: Bluurgghhh!

Tape: And that it's time to stop Time Surgeon. That it's time to STOP. God wants this to END.

He has asked me. To ask you. To turn him off.

<END>
<Outro: God plays the drums>

GOD: Oh-bop-she-bam.

<END>

Giantbum

BY

NATHANIEL MELLORS

(2008)

Two-channel video installation with animatronic sculpture. Recorded in HDV.

Produced with the support of The Centro Cultural Montehermoso, the Rijksakademie van Beeldende Kunsten, the Arts Council of England, Leeds Metropolitan University, Grizedale Arts & The A Foundation.

Giantbum — Stage 1 (rehearsal)

CAST

Narrator 1—*Sally O'Reilly*
Narrator 2—*Caroline Clifford*
Sir Boss—*Gwendoline Christie*
The Truthcurator—*David Birkin*
Sub-Priest—*Sebastian Roach*
The Father—*Johnny Vivash*
The Group—*all of the above*
Director—*Nathaniel Mellors*
Runner—*Rose Brierley*
Lights—*Matt Lippiatt*
Camera Operator A—*Stephen Folorunsho*
Camera Operator B—*Michael Smythe*
Camera Operator C—*Maria Benjamin*
Camera Operator D—*Dan Fox*
Camera Operator E—*Erkka Nissinen*

Giantbum — Stage 2 (theatre)

CAST

Sir Boss—*Gwendoline Christie*
The Father—*Johnny Vivash*
The Truthcurator—*David Birkin*
Sub-Priest—*Sebastian Roach*
(Narrators—*Sally O'Reilly & Bob Parks*)
The Group (voice only)—*all of the above*

Narrator 1: Giantbum, 1213 AD. A group of explorers…

Narrator 2:…numbering 103 people and lead by Sir Boss and his deputy The Truthcurator

Narrator 1: is lost *inside* the *backside* of an enormous Giant.

Narrator 2:…the intestinal region…

Narrator 1: *lost* inside the *very* big bum of a *very* big Giant.

Narrator 2: A *sleeping* Giant, whose mouth the adventurers had mistaken for a cave

Narrator 1: and temporary shelter.

Narrator 2: They trampled on his tongue

Narrator 1: and the giant rolled over and swallowed the entire

Narrator 2: party without waking up.

Narrator 1: Supplies are running low. The group awaits the return of their religious leader—'The Father', who has undertaken to search for a way out on behalf of the group.

Narrator 2: This was a voluntary gesture made by a fully-socialised human being.

Narrator 1: 1!2!3!4!5!6!7!8!

Narrator 2: Days pass. The group is on the verge of giving up all hope of The Father's safe return.

Narrator 1: Only Sir Boss is well-fed and taken care of.

Sir Boss: Cheers!

<Sir Boss drinks excessively and with exaggerated pleasure, spilling water down his front>

Sir Boss: Grghhhgrwhahhggrgle *<through mouth of water 'mmm this wine is really good'>* CRIKEY THAT'S GOOD WINE! Is that the Bandol? Could you pass me the rest of that smoked crane? Yes—on a cracker. That's great.

The The Truthcurator: Sir Boss. Will you let us have some? Please—and in the name of God!? WE—HAVE—NO—FOOD left unturned by the pestilential vapours from this Giant's stomach & bum-gut. Look!

<Cut to—Narrators under glass positioned like a table, being peed on by Sub-Priest>

Narrator 1: *The Sub-Priest*
Narrator 2: Not to be confused with The Father, The Sub-Priest is The Father's sinister-looking assistant
Narrator 1: *has been reduced to making wee wee drinks for the servants.*
Narrator 2: What do you think? *<whispering>* Is this a cordial situation?

Sub-Priest: Well what we are trying to do here, is I am seeking to rehydrate our capacity for escape. *We* are seeking to develop and also promote the *idea* of escape, but to stay in a hydrate state. To which end I have identified a sequential of aims: Number 1!

Narrator 1: Extenuating individualism, purpose and ambition!
Sub-Priest: Number 3!
Narrator 2: To provide the information on enabling escape required for contribution to our survival.
Sub-Priest: Number 4!
Narrator 1: To give scope to overgrow and exercise control in the actualisation of our escape from Giantbum.

Sir Boss: Cheers!

<Sir Boss drinks excessively and with exaggerated pleasure, spilling water down his front >

Sir Boss: Grghhhgrwhahhggrgle*<through mouth of water>* Crikey that's good wine! Is that the Bandol? Can you pass me the rest of that smoked crane? Yes, on a cracker. That's great.

The Truthcurator: *<enters stage as he speaks>* Sir Boss. Sir Boss. Will you let us have some? Please. In the name of God, we-have-no-food left unturned by the pestilential vapours of this giant's stomach and bum-gut. Look!
<gestures at Sub-Priest, who is urinating onto thirsty narrators>
Is this a cordial situation?
Sir Boss, will you now concede that we should indeed have beaten a path from the region of the teeth, upwards—and to the mouth—and out—and that your assertion that 'stale air always signifies an exit'…

Sub-Priest: Number 5!
Narrator 2: Drinking lots. We must drink lots to enable our existing culture to become more escape-orientated and aligned with our vision of ultimately not being in the giant bum.
Sub-Priest: Number 7!
Narrator 2: To place more emphasis on the individual's potential for escape objectives and behaviours and patterns of recognition of structured and planned development behaviour in the direction of escape!

The Truthcurator: *<steps forward, smiling, pleased with 'his' joke>* Is this a cordial situation? *<Pause. Suddenly frightened>*
The group is starving to death! How are we going to find an exit?

<Scream!>

The Father: Exit! Exit! Exit! Exit! Exit! Exit! Exit! Exit! Exit! *<different tones and volumes>*

Sir Boss: Father, is that you?

The Father: It is! I cannot come out!

The Truthcurator: Come out Father, we really appreciate you going down into the Giant's bowels, to try and find the way out for us!

Sir Boss: Come—out—Father!

The Father: I am MUCH CHANGED!

Sir Boss: What?

The Father: I have been born-again. You may not recognise me. I have become something else. In the Giant's lower intestine I became something else.

Sir Boss: You mean?

Sir Boss: <*interrupts*> It does!

The Truthcurator: well—in this *particular* instance…has proven…incelement…unfruitful…untruthful even!?

Sir Boss: <*gestures him away*>

The Truthcurator: <*suddenly frightened*> The group is starving to death! How are we going to find an exit?

The Father: <*from a dark corner at the back of the theatre*> EXIT! EXIT! EXIT! EXIT! <*repeats; different tones and volumes*>

Sir Boss: Father, is that you?

Sir Boss: Come out Father!

The Truthcurator: Come out Father, we really appreciate you going down into the bowels of the Giant to try and find the way out for us!

Sir Boss: Come—out—Father!

The Father: I am MUCH CHANGED!

Sir Boss: What?

The Father: I have been… born-again—you may not recognise me. I have become—something else. In this Giant's lower intestine—I became—something else.

Sir Boss: You mean?

The Father: Yes! I have become faecal. Feral! I mean feral! I have become feral!
<The Father emerges, black eyed, black mouth covered, chocolate substance around mouth, black lips>

Sir Boss: Oh God.

The Truthcurator: Father ! You look…really rather well!

Sir Boss: Yes, very well indeed Father. Father have you put on weight?

The Father: Exit! Exit! Exit!

Sir Boss: Did you find the exit?

The Father: Exit! Exit!

Sir Boss: Father, how did you survive? What have you been eating?

The Father: This is a bad place. Bad place. This is a bad place bum. Bad place bad bum place.

The Truthcurator: Right—no more listening to The Father everyone…. he's come back mad!

The Father: Bad bum bad bum bad bum bad bum.

The Truthcurator: Do you think he's mad, Sir Boss?

Sir Boss: No.

The Father: Bad bum bad bum bad bad bum
<looks expectantly at Sir Boss>

The Father: Yes! I have become faecal. Feral! I mean feral… I have become feral!
<The Father emerges from corner of theatre, dark eyed, chocolate substance around mouth, dark lips, hair gel, white body stocking. At a distance from Sir Boss and Truthcurator, who stand about 3 metres apart>

Sir Boss: Oh God.

The Truthcurator: Father ! You look…really rather well actually!

Sir Boss: Yes—very well indeed. Father, have you put on weight?

The Father: Exit! Exit! Exit! Exit!

Sir Boss: Father—how did you survive? What have you been eating?

The Father: This is a bad place. Bad place. Place bum place bad place place bum place bum bad place bad place bad place bad place…

The Truthcurator: Right—no more listening to The Father everyone—he's come back completely mad!

The Father: Bad bum bad bum bad…

The Truthcurator: Do you think he's mad, Sir Boss?

Sir Boss: No.

The Father: Bad bum bad bum bad bum bad bum (bad bum)
<repeat 27 times>

Sir Boss: No he's faking.

Father! Is there something you want to tell us? Feel free!

The Father: I…found…things. There is a dense forest in this Giant's sigmoidal tract over which an unholy moon casts long shadows. And in a clearing in the undergrowth at the edge of the forest I happened upon a primitive beast, who was fashioning a pair of shin-pads from the bark of a tree. I took it for a homunculus or Christian bear. This kindly spirit warned me not to venture further as the forest there is populated by savages. Cannibals! And these savages are the guardians of the Giant's brmmhmm! <*hand in mouth*> They protect his rear end from the inside-out!

Sir Boss: Now Father do you really expect us to believe that? Chinnie-reck-on! Tutankhamun! Jimmy Hill! This really is rather suspicious.

The Father: <*shouting abstractedly into the air*> The TRUTH is its own DEFENCE!

Sir Boss: No. He's faking.

Father! Is there something you want to tell us? Feel free!

The Father: <*reflective*> I…found….things. There is a dense forest in this Giant's sigmoidal tract over which an unholy moon casts a long shadow. And by a clearing, in the undergrowth at the edge of this forest I happened upon a primitive creature, who was fashioning a pair of shin-pads from the bark of a tree. I took it for a homunculus or Christian bear.

The Truthcurator: <*innocently*> Father, what did the monkey look like?

The Father: The Homunculus, Truthcurator, looked like a small, furry…. woman! With huge…black eyes—backwards eyes—and paws and wings!

The Truthcurator: <*looks really confused*>

Sir Boss: <*exasperated arm movements*>

The Father <*ignoring them*>**:** This kindly spirit warned me not to venture into the forest as it is populated by monstrous savages—cannibals! These savages are the guardians of the Giant's <*hand in mouth*> brmmhggngng-hmmm! They protect his rear end—from the inside-out!

Sir Boss: Now Father do you really expect us to believe that? Chinnie-reck-on! Tutankhamun! Jimmy Hill! This is very suspicious.

The Father: <*Shouting abstractedly into the air*> The TRUTH is its own DEFENCE!

The Truthcurator: Father, what did the monkeyness do next?

The Father: I tried to proceed beyond her—and she became savage—and flew up from the ground—as if to throttle me! I can only think she wished to save me…to save me from the cannibals! *After that I came back here straight away.*

I saw them in the trees and furtling in the bracken, banging and crackling with their bones.

My feeling of REPULSION <*as he speaks Sub-Priest draws diagram on wall with words: 'feeling'— 'REPULSION'— 'SYMPATHY'— 'REPULSION' –' PLOPPEN!'*> was magnified by SYMPATHY—these black and star-crossed unfortunates are walking waste material. Neither dead nor undead, they are faecal zombies, partially digested but also part living souls, and beyond salvation or redemption. The homunculus referred to them as… THE PLOPPEN!

Sir Boss: <*sarcastically*> Oh no, not The Ploppen!?

The Truthcurator: <*missing the sarcasm*> Oh no, not The Plopoppen! This is awful for us! And a luckless situation for the Plopoppen too.

The Father: <*irritated*> For *The Ploppen*, Truthcurator—they are called *The Ploppen!*

Sir Boss: Truthcurator—I fear these cannibals are The Father's own children! That is to say—a projection of his mind! He looks a bit…guilty. Perhaps's he's trying to…*externalise something?* Now Father! What have you been eating?

The Father: <*distressed*> There was nothing left to eat! Because of The Ploppen. I did not see the exit! Because I had to ask myself questions. What can I eat? What can I eat? If you eat yourself—eat yourself—do you *shit*

The Truthcurator: Crikey—so—you did escape the cannibals then?

The Father: I saw them in the trees…and furtling in the bracken, banging and crackling with their bones.

<suddenly pulling up a chair from no-where and sitting>

My feeling of REPULSION *<Sub-Priest write this word on blackboard>* was magnified by SYMPATHY—these black and star-crossed unfortunates are walking waste material. Neither dead nor un-dead, they are faecal zombies, partially digested but also part living souls, and beyond salvation or redemption. The Homunculus referred to them as…THE PLOPPEN!

<Sub-Priest writes words / diagram in this order: 'feeling'—REPULSION—SYMPATHY—REPULSION—PLOPPEN—with chalk on a blackboard, on the other side of the stage to The Father>

Sir Boss: *<sarcastically>* Oh no, not The Ploppen!?

The Truthcurator: *<missing the sarcasm>* Oh no, not The Plopoppen ! This is awful for us! And a luckless situation for the Plopoppen, too.

<rising from chair, correcting him>

The Father: For *The Ploppen*, Truthcurator. They are called The Ploppen!

Sir Boss: Truthcurator, I fear these cannibals are The Father's own children—that is to say, a projection of his mind. He looks a bit…*guilty*. Perhaps he's trying to…*externalise* something? Now Father! What have you been eating?

The Father: *<walking, staggering forwards as he speaks—cameras follow>* There was nothing left to eat! Because of The Ploppen. I did not see the exit! Because I had to ask myself questions. What can I eat? What can I

yourself? And what do starving cannibals eat, when they have eaten themselves? Themselves themselves? Reissue…feedback! I'm on a loop! And if you have eaten with Ploppen, do you become Ploppen, automatically?!

Sir Boss: And did you…'become Ploppen', dear Father? Is that what you'd like to tell us? Is that what you want us to know?

The Father: No!! No!! It's not true! Arrggggggghhhh! Must resist! Argghhhhhhfghdgghhh! <*shouting at his own pants*> Resist! Aghhghghghghghghhhhhhhhh! <*begins attacking his own arse area then collapses*> Get back in! Get back inside! Get back inside! Get—back—inside!!! Ngggghhhh.

<*sitting*> Godgifu! Godgyfu! Godgifu!

BRRRRPPPPPPPRRPRPPRPPRPRPRPRP!!! Oh no!

Sir Boss: I fear The Father's diet has seen him give birth to himself.

The Truthcurator: He's been born again?

Sir Boss: In a way, yes.

The Truthcurator: How wonderous! He'll be able to lead us now won't he? For did not Dionysos carry poo in his leg?

Sir Boss: No Truthcurator, Dionysos did not carry poo in his leg.

The Truthcurator: Are you sure Dionysos did not carry poo in his leg?

Sir Boss: Yes. Dionysos was born a surrogate from inside his father's leg after his mother had died. There was absolutely no poo involved.

eat? If I eat myself—eat myself—do I shit myself? And what do starving cannibals eat, when they have eaten themselves? Themselves themselves? Reissue…feedback! I'm on a loop! And if you have eaten with Ploppen, do you become Ploppen, automatically?!

Sir Boss: And did you…'become Ploppen', dear Father? Is that what you'd like to tell us? Is that what you want us to know?

The Father: No!! No!! It's not true. Arrgggggghhhh! Get back! Get back! <*shouting at his own arse-area*> Argghhhhhhfghdgghhh! Must resist! Must resist! Aghhghhh! Get back! Back, back, back inside! Get—back. Back—back—back inside! <*attacking his own arse area, then collapsing on the floor*> Aaaaghhhhhhooooogghhhhhh! Oh no! Hello again, foul shitten that doth fill my pouch and clog my tailpipe! Aaaahhh! Take that! That! Take that! Ahhhhh!

Sir Boss: I fear The Father's diet has seen him give birth to himself.

The Truthcurator: You mean he's been born again?

Sir Boss: In a way, yes.

The Truthcurator: How wonderous! Surely he'll lead us now? For did not Dionysos carry poo in his leg?

Sir Boss: No Truthcurator, Dionysos did not carry poo in his leg.

The Truthcurator: Are you sure Dionysos did not carry poo in his leg?

The Father: <*Sitting upright and talking to pants*> Godgifu! Godgyfu! Godgifu!

Sir Boss: Yes. Dionysos was born a surrogate from inside his father's leg after his Mother had died. There was absolutely no poo involved.

The Truthcurator: Near to some poo?

Sir Boss: Shhh. Now what did you eat, Father? Did you resort to eating some things you shouldn't?

The Father: No! I never did!

Freely I undertook this mission for our salvation. *Freely* I starved half to death,

Sir Boss: And *freely* you ate your own bum-cake?

The Father: I waded in effluence for days. The soft corridors narrowed and folded around me like a maze—serpentine, sluiced, swimming in slime. It was a confusing time.

Sir Boss: This is unbelievably disingenuous and annoying! Just how confusing was it Father?

The Father: We are lost in Satan's jacksie! And I have swum lengths therein!

The Group: No!

The Father: Fear not the people! For I realise now that we are *not* lost inside Satan's Jacksie!

The Truthcurator: Father—why do The Ploppen eat each other?

The Truthcurator: Near to some poo?

Sir Boss: Shhh. Now what did you eat, Father? Did you resort to eating some things you shouldn't?

The Father: No! I never did. *<picking himself up from floor>*

Freely I undertook this mission for our salvation. *Freely* I starved half to death,

Sir Boss: And *freely* you ate your own bum-cake?

The Father: *<produces a folded piece of paper from his pocket, reads from it>*
In this Giant's lower intestine I waded in effluence for—*days.*
The soft corridors narrowed and folded around me like a—*maze*
Serpentine, sluiced, swimming in *slime.*
It was a confusing *time.*

I said to myself—'Who can be behind this?'
Stan? *<looks confused, re-reads line>*
Satan?
Who can be behind this? Satan? Satan. We are lost inside Satan's jacksie.
And I have swum lengths therein!

Group: Nooooo!

The Father: *<suddenly slightly less pathetic, noticing group response>*
Fear not the people! For I realise now that we are *not* LOST INSIDE SATAN'S JACKSIE!

Group: *<no response>*

The Truthcurator: Father—why do The Ploppen eat each other?
<The Father—suddenly now with arm extensions, reaching for The Truthcurator>

The Father: The Ploppen eat each other because there is nothing else left to eat.

The Truthcurator: But then we'll never escape—if the exit is guarded by monsters...cannibals? We're doomed!

Sir Boss: We're not bloody doomed! There's only one monster here, and he is being sculptural with the truth. And not just with the truth, but with himself. Look at his arms. They are not real. He has eaten them and then made them again—out of his own shit! Look how rubbish they are! They look really unconvincing. Don't you see how he's survived? He has *regenerated* himself. He could live forever like that. Born again and in small stages!

The Truthcurator: Good God, he's living sculpture! This is like Pygmalion—but worse!
He cannot lead us anymore, his position is untenable.

Sir Boss: We must question him back in the direction of what has *REALLY HAPPENED!*

The Truthcurator: *<approaches The Father, who's arms are swinging round in circles>* Father, is there no way out for The Ploppen?

<Sir Boss brings hand to forehead in desperation>

The Father: Deliverance, you mean deliverance? Deliverance comes only to those lucky few who have been expelled from the forest during intermittent earthquakes of intra-rectal pressure!

The Truthcurator: They cease to exist?

The Father: Spiritually and physically. Their souls are TERMINATED.

The Father: The Ploppen eat each other because there is nothing else left to eat.

The Truthcurator: But then we'll never escape—if the exit is guarded by monsters...cannibals? We're doomed!

<The Father moving around with long arms>

Sir Boss: We're not bloody doomed! There's only one monster here, and he is being sculptural with the truth. And not just with the truth, but with himself. Look at his arms. They are not real. He has eaten them and then made them again—out of his own shit! Look at how rubbish they are! They look really unconvincing. Don't you see how he's survived? He has *regenerated* himself. He could live forever like that. Born again and in small stages!

The Truthcurator: Good God, he's living sculpture! This is like Pygmalion—but worse!
He cannot lead us anymore, his position is untenable.

Sir Boss: We must question him back in the direction of WHAT HAS REALLY HAPPENED!

The Truthcurator: Father, is there no way out for The Ploppen?

<Sir Boss brings hand to her forehead in desperation>

<The Father with long arms swinging>

The Father: Deliverance, you mean deliverance? Deliverance comes only to those lucky few who have been expelled from the forest during intermittent earthquakes of intra-rectal pressure!

The Truthcurator: You mean they cease to exist?

The Father: Spiritually and physically. Their souls are TERMINATED.

Sir Boss: Is this not a relief for them, from their poo-tinged cannibalism?

The Father: You mock me? Have you ever been confronted by a destiny such as mine…theirs? Ours? This looping purgatory of <*reaches into trousers*>…urghh…
I cannot..help..myself…<*produces object, eats*> I am..so ashamed…get back! get back!

<*extending hand to Truthcurator*> I have done something. I am so sorry.

The Truthcurator: Please, tell us more about The Ploppen.

The Father: They become cannibals and it is a short step from cannibalism to —

Sir Boss: Recycling?

The Father: You should have sympathy for The Ploppen! They are… Brggggh! No! Get back! Get back! Get back inside my trousers!

Who is hungry?

Group: Me! Me! Me!

The Father: Who is thirsty?

Group: Me! Me! Me!

Sir Boss: Is this not a relief for them, from their poo-tinged cannibalism?

<The Father's arms stop swinging>

The Father: Have you ever been confronted by a destiny such as mine… theirs? Ours? This looping purgatory of…*<reaches into trousers—produces object>*
I cannot..help..myself…I am…so ashamed…*<eats and extends hand towards mouth of horrified looking Truthcurator>*

I have done something. I am sorry.

The Truthcurator: *<looking horrified>* Tell us more about The Ploppen!

The Father: They became cannibals…and it is a short step from cannibalism to —

Sir Boss: Recycling?

The Father: *<angrily>* You should have sympathy for The Ploppen! They…

Bah! No! *<to his arse area>* Get back! No! *<bashes himself>* Get back! Get back! Get back inside my trousers!

<struggles with himself and retrieves himself, throwing arms outwards, losing arm extensions>

The Father: Who is hungry?

Group: Me! Me! Me!

The Father: Who is thirsty?

Group: Me! Me! Me!

The Father: Then listen to me. I THINK I CAN EXPLAIN EVERYTHING!

<becoming emotional> In the forest I was approached by one Ploppen—'Ploppen One'—who observed my religious clothing.
<emphasises his clothing>
He took me for his leader and…*<begins weeping>*

Sir Boss: Oh not again. MEN! Bring me my lunch.

The Father: The Ploppen then did kneel and chant and offer up prayers in my direction. And I was so appalled and enraged by these cannibals' composite blasphemy that I began to brandish my crucifix at them, and offer up votives to the Holy Family, but! I caught a smaller Ploppen by mistake behind his ear and his head folded, compressed and mushroomed up like a muffin, leaking whoosh! And sweet smelling brown jam. It sprayed into my mouth by accident, by God's Grace I tasted it and found it bitter but *delicious*– like manna or spish-spash! And so I discovered by happenchance, that this brown residual tribe have HEAVENLY PROPERTIES! The Ploppen taste delicious!

And lo—munching on a bum-hole guardian, I experienced a sudden and violent realisation.

The Truthcurator: An epiphany?

The Father: Yes! And I saw the answer to a number of unframed questions—

Question 1: Why is it impossible for us to find a way out of the giant?

Sir Boss: Because the giant has no perineum? Erm, he's just like a big pillow, with no arms or legs or holes! No—sorry—I mean because he's already outside.

The Father: Then—listen—to—me. I THINK I CAN EXPLAIN EVERYTHING!

<Father gains additional rubber bald-cap-head-piece>

In the forest I was approached by one Ploppen—'Ploppen One'—and he observed my religious clothing *<emphasises his clothing>* and took me for his leader *<begins weeping>*...

Sir Boss: Oh not again. Men! Bring me my lunch. Lunch! Men!?

The Father: The Ploppen then did kneel, and chant, and offer up prayers in my direction. And I was so appalled and enraged by these cannibals' composite BLASPHEMY that I began to brandish my crucifix at them *<brandishes matchstick crucifix, sets it alight with cigarette lighter>* and offer up votives to the Holy Family, but!—I caught a smaller Ploppen by mistake behind the ear and his head folded, compressed and mushroomed up like a muffin, leaking—whoosh—and sweet smelling brown jam. It sprayed into my mouth—by accident—by God's Grace I tasted it and found it bitter.... but *delicious*– like Manna or Spish-Spash!—and so I discovered by happenchance, that this brown residual tribe have HEAVENLY PROPERTIES! The Ploppen taste delicious!

And Lo—munching on a Brmrm-mah-murmur, I experienced a sudden and violent realisation.

The Truthcurator: An...epiphany?

The Father: Yes! And I saw the answer to a number of unframed questions—

Question 1: Why is it impossible for us to find a way out of the giant?

Sir Boss: Because the giant has no perineum? Because he's just like a big pillow, with no arms or legs or holes! No—sorry—it's because he's already outside.

The Father: No! We cannot find a way outside because this Giant *has no outside!*

Question 2: So how can this Giant have no outside?

Sir Boss: Erm, because we can't see the outside. No! I mean because we can't *visualise* it, *think* it I mean! No because we've forgotten it, we've forgotten what it looks like. Urggghhh! No! I mean—I mean I *know* I mean—I know! It's because we don't have any string. We don't have any string…long enough…to measure…the outside…of the….bum.

The Father: <*smiling*> Ooooh—almost Sir Boss, but sorry, NO. The Giant has no outside because IT IS THE OUTSIDE!

Question 3: How can this Giant be the outside and inside AT THE SAME TIME?

The Father: Question 3. How can this Giant be the outside and inside AT THE SAME TIME?

Sir Boss: Because we are all here? Because both occupy the same space… and are made of really small things—made out of dust and…ether…and… similar bits of…because I can't prove it isn't? Because it is, then? If I think it isn't?

The Father: Oooh, close, close! In truth there is only one way this Giant can be the outside and the inside at the same time. And we have no need for transcendental theoretical explanations or magic to explain it! Oh you lucky, lucky people. We are trapped, not just in the bowels of *an ordinary* Giant. We are trapped in the bowels of….GOD!!

The Father: Yes. <*clapping monosyllables*> It is in God that I have come to know that we are trapped! <*spits and dribbles this last syllable*>

The Group: Ooooohhh.

The Father No! We cannot find a way outside because this Giant *has no outside!*

Question 2: So how can this Giant have no outside?

Sir Boss: Because we can't see the outside. Because we can't *visualise* it, *think* it I mean! No! It's because we've forgotten it, we've forgotten what it looks like. Urggghhh! No! I mean—I *know, I know it,* I *know, I know it,* It's because we haven't got any string. We haven't got any string…long enough…to measure…the outside…of the….bum.

The Father: Ooooh—almost Sir Boss, but sorry, NO. The Giant has no outside because IT IS THE OUTSIDE!

Question 3: How can this Giant be the inside and outside AT THE SAME TIME?

<Sir Boss looks stressed and annoyed with herself>

Sir Boss: Because we are all here? Because we all occupy the same space… and are made of really small things—made out of dust and… ether…and… similar bits of…because I can't prove it isn't? Because it is, then? If I think it isn't?

The Father: Oooh, close, close! In truth there is only one way this Giant can be the inside and outside at the same time, and we have no need for transcendental theoretical explanations or magic to explain it! Oh you lucky, lucky people. We are not trapped in the bowels of *an ordinary* Giant…

We are trapped in the bowels of—GOD!!

The Father: Yes. <*clapping monosyllables*> It is in God that I have come to know that we are trap-ped! <*spits and dribbles this last syllable*>

The Father: Four. Why then, why do the walking poo-people—The Ploppen—represent our last chance of redemption?

Because without these Ploppen we would battle through the giant corpus unchallenged—only to become literally 'no-thing', nothing. Shat out by God!

The Group: Noooooo!!!

The Father: Five. Is the function of The Ploppen similar to that of an inverted contraceptive device or an intra-intestinal fishing net?
Anyone, anyone?
Yes. YES! In answer to my question, the answer is 'Yes'! The Ploppen *are* an inverted contraceptive device placed up God's bum by Jesus. This has been done, as I say, to prevent our expulsion ad nihil—into the void and screaming silence of non-existence, where there is no time and no infinity either.

So bless the Ploppen!

The Group: Bless The Ploppen!

The Father: Bless The Ploppen!

The Group: Bless The Ploppen!

The Father: Bless The Ploppen! *<physically spinning with arms out>* Bless The Ploppen! Just as God re-launched himself as Jesus as a sort of 'second chance' for everybody that had ignored Him the first time, so Jesus, now, in His empathy for our condition has modernised himself—INTO SOME POO!

The Group: Some POO!

The Father: Super-human poo!

So bless The Ploppen! And bless The Ploppen!

The Father: Four. Why then, why do the walking poo-people—The Ploppen—offer us our last chance of redemption? Anyone? Anyone?

Because without the Ploppen we would have to battle through this giant corpus unchallenged—only to become 'no-thing', nothing. Shat out by God!

The Father: Five. Is the function of The Ploppen similar to that of an inverted contraceptive device? Anyone, anyone?
Yes. YES! In answer to my question, the answer is 'Yes'! The Ploppen *are* an inverted contraceptive device placed up God's bum by Jesus
to prevent our expulsion into the void and screaming silence of non-existence, where there is no time and no infinity either.

So bless the Ploppen! Bless The Ploppen!

The Father: Just as God *re-launched* himself as Jesus as a sort of 'second chance' for all those who had ignored him, so Jesus, now, in His *empathy* for our condition has *modernised* himself—INTO SOME POO!

The Group: Some POO!

The Father: Super human poo!

The Group: Bless The Ploppen!

The Father: So Bless The Ploppen! Bless the Ploppen!

The Group: Bless The Ploppen!

The Father: They are Christ's foot-soldiers! Earth's angels! Essential and flavoursome multiplication of Saviour!

The Group: Spin! Spin! Spin!

The Father: Jesus is the gynaecologist of God's bum!

The Group: Bum! Bum! Bum! Bum! Bum! Bum! Bum! Bum! Bum! Bum!

The Father: His humanisation is complete!

The Group: *<SILENCE>*

******

The Truthcurator: Oh bless The Ploppen! The Ploppen are Buggering Heroes in my book!

Sir Boss: *<slaps and repeatedly punches Truthcurator in face>*

The Truthcurator: Ow! Oooh! Ow!

Sir Boss: Truthcurator! Sort. Your. Brain. Out. The Father's story is riddled with inconsistencies and giant swooping fruit loops. It is patent NON-SENSE. Listen to what he's saying—'The Ploppen are guarding the exit but there is no outside because we are in God's bum?'?! Jesus has reincarnated Himself as a super-human race of excremental cannibals to *save* us from getting out of here? Truthcurator! We WANT TO GET OUT OF HERE! This is bad. We cannot lose our leadership to a mad monk with a poo-fetish and the ability to frighten everyone into following him. Now snap out of it and help me to help us out!

The Father: *<physically spinning around with arms out>* So Bless The Ploppen!
Bless the Ploppen! They are Christ's footsoldiers! Earth's angels! Essential and flavoursome multiplication of Saviour!

The Group: Spin! Spin! Spin!

The Father: Jesus is the gynaecologist of God's bum!

The Group: Bum! Bum! Bum! Bum! Bum! Bum! Bum! Bum! Bum! Bum!

The Father: His *humanisation* is complete!

The Group: *<SILENCE>*

******

The Truthcurator: Oh bless The Ploppen! The Ploppen are buggering heroes in my book!

<Sir Boss punches Truthcurator in the face.>

The Truthcurator: Ow!

Sir Boss: Truthcurator! Sort. Your. Brain. Out. The Father's story is riddled with inconsistencies and giant great swooping fruit loops. Just listen to what he's telling you — 'The Ploppen are guarding the exit but there is no way out because we are trapped in God's bum?'?! Jesus has reincarnated Himself as a super-human race of excremental cannibals to *save* us from getting out of here? Truthcurator! We WANT TO GET OUT OF HERE! This is bad. Bad! We cannot lose our leadership to a mad monk with a poo-fetish and the ability to frighten everyone into following him. Now snap out of it and help me to help us out!

The Father: *<moving mechanically> This* is our third strike. *They* are our last-chance-salon. Because through the example of their feckless and fetid auto-munchery they instruct us to 'Go back! Go back and be absorbed into God's fundament!'
This is our third strike. *They* are our last-chance-salon.
Because through the example of their feckless and fetid auto-munchery they instruct us to 'Go back! Go back and be absorbed into God's fundament!'

The Truthcurator: *<suddenly seeing things from Sir Boss' point of view>* Oh what fresh madness is this? The Father is a coprophiliac? And to make matters worse he is elaborating a metaphysical system based on falling into some sewage? We are inside a Giant, aren't we, Sir Boss? This is real and not a metaphysic?

Sir Boss: *<pats Truthcurator, reassuringly>* Of course we are Truthcurator, of course. Somewhere inside this Giant's plumbing, The Father's mind has been bent.

The Truthcurator: Our own Father, working against us! How can this happen? This is like Hell! For things like this to happen; nature reversed. Are we in Hell Sir Boss?

The Father: Not Hell but next to Heaven!!

Sir Boss: Oh for fuck's sake we are not in Hell or Heaven. We are stuck inside a Giant's arsehole. That—is—our—situation. Now. Is there another human being left in this theatre with any memory of reality?

The Father: We are just a short walk from Heaven!

We have been eaten!

Group: TEMPORAL! TEMPORAL!

The Father: *This* is our third strike. *They* are our last-chance-salon. Because through the example of their feckless and fetid auto-munchery they instruct us to 'Go back! Go back and be absorbed into God's fundament!'

Truthcurator: <*looking increasingly irritated and angry during the above speech, he has been turned*> Oh! What fresh madness is this!? The Father has become a coprophiliac? And to make matters WORSE he is elaborating a metaphysical system based on falling into some sewage? We ARE inside a Giant, aren't we, Sir Boss? This is real, not a metaphysic?

Sir Boss: <*reassuringly*> Of course we are Truthcurator, of course. Deep inside this Giant's plumbing The Father's mind has been bent.

The Truthcurator: Our own Father, working against us! How can this happen? Oh. This is like Hell! For things like this to happen. Nature—reversed! Are we in Hell, Sir Boss?

The Father: <*shouting*> Not Hell but next to Heaven!!

Sir Boss: Oh for fuck's sake we are not in Hell or Heaven. We are trapped inside a Giant's arse-hole. That—is—our—situation. Now. Is there another human being left in this theatre with any memory of reality?

The Father: We are just a short walk from Heaven!
Group: Heaven!

The Father: We have been eaten!

Group: Temporal! Temporal!

The Father: We MUST be digested !

Group: Purified!

The Father: In order to be…

Group: PURIFIED!!

The Father: Yes! Our souls are but Christ's lunch inside God's bum!

Group: BUM! BUM! BUM! *<repeats at different speeds>*

THE END

The Truthcurator: We need to undermine him—he is fucking their heads in!

The Father: We are blessed! These are God's own meadow muffins! Eat! Dance! Join together!

The Truthcurator: Sir Boss!? We need to undermine him, he is *really* fucking their heads in!

The Father: We must eat them and ourselves be eaten by them. Thus shall we be absorbed—into the bum-gut of The Lord!

Sir Boss: He has wowed them with his vertical logic. God is behind… this…behind…this is fatal…fatal!

The Truthcurator: He got me there too for a minute. But you helped me see it from your point of view. Sir Boss, what is your perspective on the ups and downs—the ins and outs—the horizontals and the verticals of this situation?

The Father: We must be digested !

Group: Purified!

The Father: In order to be…

Group: Killed! Killed and saved!

The Father: Yes! Our souls are but Christ's lunch inside God's bum!

THE END

Sir Boss: He has wowed them with his vertical logic. God is behind… this…behind…this is fatal…fatal!

The Truthcurator: He had me there too for a minute. But you helped me see it from your point of view. Sir Boss, what is your perspective on the ins and outs, the ups and downs, the horizontals and the verticals of the whole situation?

Sir Boss: My perspective is diagonal. Nonetheless since man got up from all fours he has been joined directly from arse to tit and is prone to see things vertically.

The Truthcurator: What are we going to do?

The Father: Who shall join me? Forwards to death and redemption!

Sir Boss: Our position is as stinky as this 'subject'. Our brightest theologian—born-again and blasphemous! Wait, that's it!

The Truthcurator: What's it Sir Boss?

Sir Boss: Their minds are rinsed with FEAR and BIG IDEAS. We must make him ABSURD! To bring him down to earth. We need just the right words *–we must call him names!*

The Truthcurator: Erm?

Sir Boss: Come on Truthcurator think! He has been freshly christened, born twice. So 'Father' alone cannot suffice—when he has multiplied thusly, he is so befouled..

The Truthcurator: Mad!

Sir Boss: And covered in smudge. Now we have Father, and Rather-More-Than Father! What shall we call this new Father, that walks in and is his own landscape?

The Father and loam? Peasant and strip? Father Plus? Father Father?

The Truthcurator: Present, unpleasant—shit! Erm...Doctor, Doctor Poo?
Sir Boss: That's good—I mean—it is like a form of time-travel—The Father being attacked by his own little Time Lords! But come on—he's carrying his own landscape—The Landlord and the pub?

Sir Boss: My perspective is diagonal. Nonetheless since man got up from all fours he has been joined directly from arse to tit and is prone to seeing things vertically.

The Truthcurator: What are we going to do?

Sir Boss: Our position is as stinky as this 'subject'. Our brightest theologian—born-again and blasphemous! Wait, that's it!

The Truthcurator: What's it? What's it Sir Boss?

Sir Boss: Their minds are rinsed with FEAR and BIG IDEAS. We need just the right words to bring him down to earth. *We must call him names*!

The Truthcurator: Erm? *<time passes>*

Sir Boss: Come on Truthcurator think! He has been freshly christened, born twice. So 'Father' alone cannot suffice—when he has multiplied thusly, he is so befouled…

The Truthcurator: Mad!

Sir Boss:…and covered in smudge. Now we have Father, and Rather-More-Than Father! What do we call this new Father who walks in and is his own landscape?

The Father and loam? Peasant and strip? Father Plus? Father Father?

The Truthcurator: Present and unpleasant—shit? Erm…Dung…dung…. dung?

Sir Boss: Father Compost, Father Cowplop, Father away from me would be preferable…

The Truthcurator: *<looks blank>* Professional....specialist...

Sir Boss: England and Englishman?

The Truthcurator: No plan...man. Upwards and sideways at the same time man?

Shit Mass! Father Shitmass!

Sir Boss: Come on Truthcurator! Bounce—the—words—with—me.

'You have the right to cup your own plop, but do not expect us to discuss the meaning of your activities—oh you! Mad and hopeful CRETIN!'

The Truthcurator: Cretin!

Sir Boss: Arch-fool!

The Truthcurator: Ch-fool!

Sir Boss: Poo-pawn!

The Truthcurator: Ping-pong!

Sir Boss: And unmutual TURD HAMMOCK!

The Truthcurator: Trachemock!

Sir Boss: Oh for God's sake Truthcurator, you are as thick as a planet.

The Truthcurator: I'm not sure this is really...

Sir Boss: Let's try something else. Let's try increasing the level of fragmentation in the dialogue—perhaps we can destroy him virally, by confusing things more than before.

The Truthcurator: *<laughs sycophantically>*

Sir Boss: *<looks irritated>*

The Truthcurator: Shit Mass! Father Shitmass!

Sir Boss: Come on Truthcurator! Bounce—the—words—with—me.

'You have the right to cup your own plop, but do not expect us to discuss the meaning of your activities—oh you! Mad and hopeful CRETIN!'

The Truthcurator: Cretin!

Sir Boss: Arch-fool!

The Truthcurator: Ch-fool!

Sir Boss: Poo-pawn!

The Truthcurator: Ping-pong!

Sir Boss: And unmutual TURD HAMMOCK!

The Truthcurator: Trachemock!

Sir Boss: Oh for God's sake Truthcurator, you are as thick as a planet.

The Truthcurator: I don't really think this is working.

Sir Boss: Let's try something else. Let's try increasing the level of fragmentation in the dialogue—perhaps we can regain control by confusing things more than before.

The Truthcurator: Narrative fragmentation fragmentation

Sir Boss: Infinity

The Truthcurator: and colour

Sir Boss: the colour yellow

The Truthcurator: representing… people

Sir Boss: mirrored, and subtracted

The Truthcurator: from infinity

Sir Boss: *abstracted* from me

The Truthcurator: minus one

Sir Boss: minus me

The Truthcurator: and in its mirror

Sir Boss: *<gesticulating as if delivering the 'magic word'>* A THIRD!

<PAUSE>

The Truthcurator: Did it work?

Sir Boss: *<head rotating as if hypnotised>* Are you still here?

The Truthcurator: Yes! No!

The Truthcurator: Narrative fragmentation fragmentation

Sir Boss: Infinity

The Truthcurator: and colour

Sir Boss: the colour yellow

The Truthcurator: representing people

Sir Boss: mirrored and subtracted

The Truthcurator: from infinity

Sir Boss: representing blue

The Truthcurator: representing greenish-red

Sir Boss: representing black, abstracted from me

The Truthcurator: minus one

Sir Boss: minus me

The Truthcurator: Did it work? *<close up of faces—David wearing veil and carrying a packed lunch, Sir Boss' fur coat is larger>*
Sir Boss: *<head rotating as if hypnotised>* Are you still here?

The Truthcurator: Yes! *<total change of tone>* N-o-oh!

Sir Boss: Everything is...exactly the same!

The Truthcurator: Everything is…almost exactly the same.

The Truthcurator: Well it's the same—but—everyone's gone!

The Truthcurator: Goodbye The Father!

Bye faithful servants! <*pause*>

We'll be fine now they've gone, won't we Sir Boss?

Sir Boss: Yes. It's much better now they've gone.

The Truthcurator: Are we all alone then?

Sir Boss: Yes.

The Truthcurator: But you're here?

Sir Boss: Yes.

The Truthcurator: And…so am I?

Sir Boss: Yes.

Sir Boss: Everything is...exactly the same!

The Truthcurator: Everything is…almost exactly the same.

Sir Boss: What do you mean?

The Truthcurator: It's the same—but—everyone's gone!

The Truthcurator: Goodbye The Father!

Goodbye faithful servants!

<PAUSE>

We'll be fine now they've gone, won't we Sir Boss?

Sir Boss: Yes. It's much better now they've gone.

The Truthcurator: Are we all alone then?

Sir Boss: Yes.

The Truthcurator: But you are here?

Sir Boss: Yes.

The Truthcurator: And…so am I?

Sir Boss: Yes

Giantbum – Stage 3 (animatronics)

BY

NATHANIEL MELLORS

Oh-oh-oh, take me with you

You! *You!*

Although I am besmirched, I have tasted freedom and it hurts
Although I am besmirched, I have tasted freedom and it hurts
Although I am besmirched, I have tasted freedom and it hurts

I may be nearly blind. Insensible even
Insensible even
Insensible even

But I can see the way from here and I hold ha ha ha hold
ha ha ha hold
ha ha ha hold
the exclusive right of freedom. Freedom, freedom, free-ee-ee-dom!
the exclusive right of freedom. Freedom, freedom, free-ee-ee-dom!
the exclusive right of freedom. Freedom, freedom, free-ee-ee-dom!

OH take WE. Me with you! Although I am besmirched. I've tasted freedom
OH take WE. Me with you! Although I am besmirched. I've tasted freedom
OH take WE. Me with you! Although I am besmirched. I've tasted freedom
A-a-a-and it hurts. It hurts. I may be nearly blind. Insensible even.
But I can see
A-a-a-and it hurts. It hurts. I may be nearly blind. Insensible even.
But I can see
A-a-a-and it hurts. It hurts. I may be nearly blind. Insensible even.
But I can see
the way from here, and I hold, hold, hold, the exclusive right to freedom. Free-ee-
the way from here, and I hold, hold, hold, the exclusive right to freedom. Free-ee-
the way from here, and I hold, hold, hold, the exclusive right to freedom. Free-ee-
dom. Free-ee-dom.
dom. Free-ee-dom.

dom. Free-ee-dom.

And hold. Hold. Hold, ha-ha-ha-ha-ha-hold The exclusive right of freedom!

Hold, ha-ha-ha-ha-ha-hold
Hold, ha-ha-ha-ha-ha-hold

Freedom, freedom, freedom!
Freedom, freedom, freedom!
Freedom, freedom, freedom!

Freedom, freedom, freedom!
Freedom, freedom, freedom!
Freedom, freedom, freedom!

Freedom, freedom, freedom!
Freedom, freedom, freedom!
Freedom, freedom, freedom!

Exit! Exit! Exit!

EXIT EXIT EXIT
EXIT EXIT EXIT

EXIT EXIT EXIT
EXIT EXIT EXIT

EXIT EXIT EXIT

EXIT!
EXIT!

EXIT!

EXIT!

EXIT!

E.
X.
I.
T.

The Preface

BY

NATHANIEL MELLORS

(2009)

Installation with animatronic sculpture and sound.

Produced as an appendix to *Giantbum*.

Commissioned by the Stedelijk Museum Bureau Amsterdam
with the financial support of the Netherlands Fund
for Visual Arts, Design and Architecture.

(I) THE PREFACE

The creator, lodged in its creation[1], footnote one:

I have been waiting for this moment for 332 years
I have been waiting for this moment for 332 years
I have been waiting for this moment for 332 years...

The impossibility of a creator outside of its creation.
The impossibility of getting out of the bloody place!

Inside the Black Egg *or* The Creator, Lodged In Its Creation

Welcome to the beginning of the end of the exhibition. I am The Preface and author of this work.

~~I have modelled the installation in a colon, and so, if you will picture a physical grammar, I occupy the full stop. Fuh! Fuh! I fashioned it and I am its tenant. I hang from it—like a bogey. I am adherent. The addition of which dangler gives my full stop the aspect of a comma, a comma with a tail of hardening mucus <,> but with a commitment to atrophy and ultimate detachment.~~

I made these heads and then they would not speak with me...they consider themselves **above** me—superior in some form. They hate me. And so I will not speak with them or look at them and have not been inside the work for aeons. I do not remember what the appearance of, er, the appearance of the faces is. I recall my own face however has slipped somewhat.

I have been waiting for this moment for 332 years
I have been waiting for this moment for 332 years
I have been waiting for this moment for 332 years
Ihavebeenwaitingforthismomentfor332years

1. Een fundament van Spinoza's monisme—de onmogelijkheid van het bestaan van een schepper buiten zijn schepping; 'Deus sive Natura'.

After 332 years of Hermetick preparation I am just about ready to drop off.

(Dutch synth: 'Preparation H.')

<Blows raspberry.>

Stuck inside this room I have laid out a set of demonstrations, in explanation of my works and thoughts. ~~Do not mistake this for an intentional act of irony. It is an expression of impotence.~~ I have been thinking about thinking. And making pictures of thought.

Demonstration 1: Demonstration of the manufacturer of the Quintessence.

Colon: a plinth.

Look at this piece of sculpture! Observe this jar. I have been masticating the head of the dead British screenplay writer Dennis Potter for some time now. Dennis is dead. And that *<points to a piece of coal in yellow liquid in a jar>* is his head. Now if you look at the head from a certain angle, and if the light catches it just so, glances upon its surface from the correct angle—you will witness a rather peculiar and wonderful visual effect—the head looks like a piece of coal. And this environment is set in coal. On. A plinth.

Synth' voice: **S for skin!**

The Murdoch-owned cryogenics laboratory has successfully reanimated the headless playwright's corpse; it floats in liquid suspension, and electricity prompts muscle memory into flailing, empty* and increasingly childish gestures of resistance—the v-sign, the bird, the coital forefinger in and out of the hole created between index finger and thumb.

<* Simultaneous voice 1:> Someone gave me the tip off and I bought it[Δ], I gave them 1500 quid for it. It tastes a bit like a toffee.
<Δ Simultaneous voice 2:> I am experiencing some pain here—I am expe-

riencing the pain of authorship.[Ω] And the insensitive prick of critical awareness.
< Ω Simultaneous voice 3:> I am masticating the smoked head of the writer, I have sucked most of it away, I have sucked it down like a gobstopper, I absorb the artist's ideas — I can soak up its patterns of thought, its ways of getting ideas. And when it becomes smaller I soak it in a suspension of alcohol and nicotine and it expands again over a few weeks, but its thoughts then are somewhat horrific, increasingly disturbed, something of a parody upon a parody (*a parody*) also quieter, they are folded in *static* and *shame.*

<*Kippen sounds*> Stuck here in this hinterland, I have achieved the benefit of a certain distance upon my creation. And the benefit of time, the passage of time over which certain objects fall out of focus, others which lacked form and definition become crystalline and acute.
Although my face has fallen off as I have became rotten, through my writing. Despite that — you will forgive any grammatical errors — these are the result of my physical deterioration.

Description of the giant bum:

I have been alone here so long I am in danger of speaking only in intransitives. *Glower, yawn, leer and piss.* WESTERN SULPHUR! ***Carbon Humanum.*** C.

C >>>

In this work there is a base confusion, between **the inside** and **the outside**. Am I inside or outside this thought? Am I inside or outside this idea? Am I inside or outside these words?

C >>>

As I became confused between the inside and outside, I realised I needed spectacles, and the spectacles I was looking through were melting — as TIME's agency <*here see my former work 'Sculpture Against Time'*> acted upon my thoughts and words. The IDEA took me a very long time, long enough for the glass to flow out of the bottom of my spectacles and onto the floor. Having had the IDEA however, the ACTION took a split-second to realise:

<Chorus: Carbon Humanum (repeats)>

- I ground the pool of glass into dust and sucked it back in through my eyeball!
- I saw my work as through a diamond contact lens. I saw my lens through a diamond contact—refracted—and I realised—I am not the author of this work, this work is the author of me.

Visions! I ground the pool of glass and sucked it back in through
my eyeball.
I experienced a vision in blind, electric pain. Visions!
Ground glass sucked in through the eyeball!
Ground glass sucked in through the eyeball!

There is still much about the molecular physics and thermodynamics of glass that is not well understood. ('I'll tell you this though—never put glass in your eyes.')

Eyes

I have taken out my eyes—boiled one and buried the other.

Number 1: The Boiled Eye* Here is a recipe for eating your eye, which improves your eyesight. Take a good beef stock—not too salty. The eye will become cloudy as it cooks, cook it properly and it will tenderise and soften—there should be no crunch of lens or sudden burst of cold cold liquid in the mouth.
Can you see better if you eat your own eyes?

< Simultaneous voice:> I have taken out my eyes—boiled one and buried the other.*
Number 1: The Boiled Eye.

Here is a recipe for eating your eye, which improves your eyesight. Take a good beef stock—not too salty. The eye will become cloudy as it cooks, cook it properly and it will tenderise and soften- there should be no crunch of lens or sudden burst of cold cold liquid in the mouth. There should be no crunch of lens or sudden burst of cold cold liquid in the mouth.

(II) The Athanor

The Buried. Oh black eyeball, the philosophic eye which I store inside
THE ATHANOR!
THE ATHANOR!
THE ATHANOR! <Het Filosofische Oog>

This is my philosopher's furnace and I have lost it!
Somewhere on the inside of this sculpture. I don't remember where precisely.
If you find it, will you bring it to me?

If you find it, will you bring it to me?—I've lost my Athanor, Athanor!
If you find it, will you bring it to —I have lost my Atha-
me? nor.

If you see it, will you bring it to me? It's on the inside there somewhere...it might be behind all the felt.

What I am presenting you with here is a performance. I feel a little nervous to perform live in explanation of my work, er…this is an outside work, so, to, er elucidate it is a model of thought, a bogey-strung model of a brain, a picture of a thought, so to speak—made out of snot. And that idea—the idea for the picture of thought, made out of snot—is in and of itself ….SNOT.

Look here at these, er, number.
This sculpture is called 'World Piece', 2000- and..
P-I-E-C. Observe!:

One bogey sculpture is illustrative of the atomic structure of coal.

The second bogey sculpture is illustrative of the atomic structure of a diamond.

And the third demonstrates Spinozan monism. It is a bogey-strung sculpture of God, appropriate for all religions. A universal solvent and proposal for world peace.

(III) ADMINISTRATOR OF THE UNIVERSE

I am a critical reader for this work. And also its author.

I am critical by nature and its reader by employment. Fear not for fright fearful shadow, for I will explain this to you clearly and without rhetoric. As its *reader*, I am the author of this work. We are in an environment where causality flows backwards as well as forwards. Very, very slowly. A affects B and the affected B affects A back, but differently for being affected. So A proceeds differently as a result of its effects on B. Thus—the environment evolves along with its contents. And so the idea of a controlled physical experiment is a nonsense without an awareness of this dimension of shift in cause and effect, this dimension of feedback, and its effect from **A** to **B** and back again to **A**, which has now become—a different **A**.

Aaaaaaaaaaaaaaaaaaaaaaaaaaaaaaaaaaaaaaaaaaaaaand back to my point > **.**

The artist is my creation.
Nathaniel Mellors is a programme, run by me. Not a very good one, I'll admit. Not a very good one, not a very good one. A very good one, not. I will say this of it however—*it's not a very good one.* Sorry—it is *appropriate* in its energy expenditure. Flailing, mildy disruptive, sometimes within its lexicon—an environment which I designed and now hold an administrative post in—an environment which I *operate* according to

a certain set of physical laws. And these laws are like plants, they need watering and tending to. They grow and change a little, as the aeons click by and the programmes like Nathaniel, *expend energy* and exert their arthritic efforts upon the environment. Through this process of feedback—this is the truly magical part—what both sides can achieve shifts and moves—so the lexicon itself changes—the environment changes—the physical laws of the environment shift. What I demonstrate here on a cellular level is also happening on a larger and larger scale, harmonically and throughout a massive patchwork omniverse. HUGIVERSE!

As I was saying I hold an administrative post in this environment, which I am also the creator of. I have a franchise—a licence—for it, and operate it according to a certain set of physical laws, which I will refer to as
A LEXICON.
Observe my plants.
To clarify, we are not lost inside Satan's bumhole, God's guts or an enormous belly of giant nostalgia, or some grammatological chamber, as if grammar were physical. We are lost inside a nasal cavity, which is a physical lexicon of which I am chief administrator, within a universe for which conventional administration is sort, of, er...possibly insubstantial. We are coming apart at an administrative level for reasons which we have discovered are in fact ontological—the universe itself is not well-suited to administration. It is not governed by a single set of rules. And so the administration that we have administered upon it sits awkwardly, it covers the cosmos like a child's bonnet on the head of a man of massive corporal distension and handicap—partially and with a rather absurd and stupid look to it. Should anyone give it a second glance.

And so we discovered we are administrating an **un-niverse.**

The rules have changed. The act of creation is a work in progress. Do not think of the big bang, think of a firework display, running forever, and each pop and crack and fizzle is the crackling emergence of a new physics within its locality, inside which new civilisations emerge, evolve and eventually die, along with the emerging and evolving physics that support them. The physics change as the participants within that physics act upon it.

And so in many ways The Father is correct. We are lost inside God's bum. And the idea of **The Ploppen** (*'Ploppen'*), if we think of them as passive agents who have in a sense turned upon their environment and become active, is not as absurd as it seems.

And finally—CONCLUSIONS:

Ruminations on titles: Now Big wanted to call this <*short, incomprehensible word*>, but I am afflicted by cynicism and allergic to rhetoric. How ironic then that I am given the job of administrating a rhetorical programme—Nathaniel—that thinks of itself as a critical agent of rhetoric *just as it promotes the phenomenon!* But I need such a creature in order to advance the rhetorical structure. So he crashes around, he may yet have something useful stuck to his legs, and so by hook or by crook, when he is not looking, probably not aware of it, he might accidentally pollinate something, get something up the stick, whether or not he is capable of taking responsibility or even half aware of his actions.

So I am describing entropy within a given area.

And so you see we are not lost inside the bowels of a Giant, we are lost inside a *cosmological nostrus*, or rather travelling inside an infinite sneeze, moving outward, expanding, a tidal wave, a sort of tidal wave of mucus, a plane of snot, a single snotty substance, a Petri dish, gelatinous-latinous 'splosion.

I realised I needed spectacles to put everything into focus at the same time.

A LENS.

I achieved this lens at the expense of my health.
If you look through my lens you may experience a vision of reality:

Everything is equally blurry.

Ourhouse

BY

NATHANIEL MELLORS

(2010–)

Incomplete at the time of this publication.

Conceived as a multi-episode video installation with animatronic sculpture. Recorded in HD.

Commissioned by De Hallen Haarlem and the British Art Show with the financial support of the Netherlands Film Fund and the Netherlands Fund for Visual Arts, Design and Architecture

CREDITS

Produced by *NOMAD*
(Michael Smythe & Piera Buckland) &
Nathaniel Mellors
Written and Directed by
Nathaniel Mellors
Story development by
Nathaniel Mellors & Dan Fox

Director of Photography: *Ben Wheeler*
1st Assistant Director: *Michael Smythe*
Camera Assistant: *Dan Brough*
Sound: *Freddy Claire, Ryan Chandler &*
Ariel Sultan
Lighting: *Shaun Moan*
Art Design: *Nathaniel Mellors*
Art Design: (Wales) *Andrew Birkin*
Art Design: (The George & Dragon)
Richardette and Lilianna Sanguino
Casting: *Gwendoline Christie &*
Nathaniel Mellors
Associate Producer: *Gwendoline Christie*
Costumes, Props & Make-up:
Nathaniel Mellors, Gwendoline Christie
& Piera Buckland
Digital Imaging Technician: *Stefan Yap*
Production Assistants: *Llewellyn Thomas,*
Amele Sumpter & Terry Smith
Executive Producers: *Xander Karskens &*
Jonty Claypole
Editing: *Nathaniel Mellors & Andy Cooke*
Original Music: *Andy Cooke*
Editor At Large: *Andrea Carnevali*
Special sound effects: *Alex Ellerington*
Additional material: *The Cast*

CAST:
The Object—*Brian Catling*
Charles Maddox-Wilson /
'Daddy'—*Richard Bremmer*
Annalise Wilson / 'Babydoll'—
Gwendoline Christie
Robert Jobson / 'Bobby Jobby'—
Johnny Vivash
Truson Maddox-Wilson—*David Birkin*
Faxon Jackson Maddox-Wilson—
Benedict Hopper
Uncle Tommy—*Patrick Kennedy*
Brian The Director—*Benedict Sandiford*
Mick Jagger—*Duke Brooks & Joe Brooks*
Mick Hucknall—*Jimmy Bradshaw*
Mick Fleetwood—*Ryan Ellsworth*
Lorraine The Pub Landlandy—
Princess Julia
Councillor 1—*Michael Smythe*
Councillor 2—*Piera Buckland*
Worker 1—*Will McGeough*
Worker 2—*Nathaniel Mellors*
Worker 3—*Stefan Yap*
Other roles t.b.c.

SCENARIO

A huge male figure, clad in pristine sportswear appears in the lounge of 'Ourhouse', the home and estate of a liberal bohemian European family. This figure sits crossed legged and still. Initially the family do not recognise it as human. They mistake it for some kind of object ('The Object') or non-human thing ('Thingy'). When they try to talk about it they experience a kind of aphasia. It becomes apparent by their divergent reactions that they are all having a different experience of 'The Object'.

'The Object' controls language within the house. At night it ingests books from the library, partially digests them and excretes them as a series of base sculptures. This causes a number of fantastical episodes to occur which the family are forced to play out. The themes of the episodes are a mixture of the ingested texts.

The appearance of The Object and the conflation of reality and fantasy that it engenders heightens tensions between the family and the outside world. This reconfigures the dynamics of the family, destroying the internal hierarchy and changing roles.

LOCATION

'Ourhouse': an English manor house and its grounds in the timeless English countryside.

Internal vs. External Space: Deliberate inconsistency between Ourhouse's external appearance, which is fixed, and its internal capacity and content, which becomes increasingly convoluted. As The Object's influence grows, the inside and the outside are conflated; pub, swimming pool, theatre, and landscape locations are manifest internally and in expanding form.

Causality: The Object is enabling a reciprocation of fantasy and reality. There is causal ambiguity between family members' behaviour and what is going on in the house. Is The Object's appearance the result of the behaviour of an individual or of the entire family or neither?

Interior characteristics: Individualist, creative, artistic, hierarchical,

hermetic, subjective, potentially elitist, analogically Royalist, self-destructive.
Exterior characteristics: Pseudo-democratic, committed to an excessive level of administration and bureaucracy, analogically Parliamentarian, self-perpetuating, homogenising.

CHARACTERS

THE MADDOX-WILSONS: A 'COMPLEX FAMILY'

1960's bohemianism, alternative educational and countercultural lifestyle models, and straight bourgeois values are in free-fall within this group. Concepts of self-realisation and liberation rub up against family responsibilities. Although seemingly a liberated extended family, it has a patriarchal centre, and follows a traditional nuclear family structure.

CHARLIE MADDOX-WILSON / 'DADDY': The patriarch and owner of Ourhouse
ANNALISE 'BABYDOLL' WILSON: Daddy's partner
FAXON JACKSON MADDOX-WILSON: Daddy's adopted son
TRUSON MADDOX-WILSON: Daddy's son
UNCLE TOMMY: Daddy's estranged alcoholic brother

THE VISITOR TO OURHOUSE

THE OBJECT: a huge mysterious figure, a powerful visitation

OTHER INHABITANTS OF OURHOUSE

Ourhouse is not just a family home, but an extension of Daddy's ego and wealth:

> ROBERT JOBSON / 'BOBBY JOBBY': family handyman and gardener—from the outside but partially internalised
> LORRAINE: landlady of the pub within Ourhouse
> THE WORKERS: supposedly engaged in 'repairs', actually a trade-union & British social history re-enactment society mistakenly employed by Daddy
> THE DRAMA GROUP: employed by Daddy to realise his ambitions as auteur, they work in the theatre within Ourhouse
> BRIAN THE DIRECTOR: director of the drama group, himself directed by Daddy
> THE THREE MICKS: MICK JAGGER, MICK HUCKNALL, MICK FLEETWOOD

THE WORLD OUTSIDE OURHOUSE

> THE CRUSTS: the neighbours, in an escalating feud with Daddy
> THE COUNCIL / 'THE SANHEDRIN': a powerful bureaucratic organisation that wishes to recruit Daddy to its ranks

Various fantastical characters generated by The Object, some of which are played by members of Daddy's family.

"EPISODE 1—GAMES"

EXT.—THE MOON AT DAWN

'The Object' has appeared with the dawn inside Ourhouse, the country home of a liberal bourgeois family. The Object is a large, threatening, male form. It sits, cross-legged, in the living-room wearing pristine sportswear. The family are not aware of its presence inside their home.

FADE IN:
EXT.—OURHOUSE

View of the building at dawn.

FOCUS IN ON FRONT-ROOM WINDOW.

A moth has settled on the interior window-pane.

INT.—LIVING-ROOM

The moth flies from the window pane about the room and settles on the cheek of The Object.

CLOSE UP OF THE OBJECT*1

The Object is completely still.

CUT TO:
INT. GROUND FLOOR ROOMS AND CORRIDORS

Truson Maddox-Wilson, wearing only underwear and trainers, is standing behind a pot-plant in the cloak-room, breathing heavily and staring intently into the middle-distance. His facebears the result of a crude attempt at camouflage make-up. He has a pair of binoculars around his neck and is holding a cheese knife which he is sharpening with a stone. He sets off along the ground floor of the house, crawling and using bits of furniture and architecture to hide behind and climb on as he progresses. He appears to be stalking something.

INT.—LIVING-ROOM & ADJACENT ROOMS
CLOSE UP OF THE OBJECT*2

The Object's iris contracts. It makes a short, slight guttural noise.

CUT TO:

Truson crawling down a corridor with his knife in his mouth, approaching the living-room.

SHOT:
HAND-HELD JUST ABOVE HIS BACK AS HE CRAWLS ALONG

CUT TO:

The Object in the foreground, the moth still on its cheek. In the background Truson crawls straight past the entrance to this room down a corridor without noticing the room or The Object.

CLOSE IN ON THE OBJECT'S FACE FOR A CLOSE-UP, HOLD FOR A FEW SECONDS AFTER TRUSON HAS PASSED.

EXT.—OURHOUSE, SIDE-VIEW

Truson bowls out of a door at the side of the house as if spat out by it. He falls into a forward-roll and stops, crouched on the lawn. He throws his knife at a nearby tree. It embeds horizontally in the bark of the trunk half-way between the ground and the first branches. Truson lets out a joyful whoop, jumps into the air and floats upwards. He has a look of intense focus as he moves vertically through the space between the grass and the tree, paddling his arms like he is swimming in the air and teetering a little as if attempting to keep balance. He alights on the lower branches of the tree and disappears into it. The tree shakes a little as he does so. Birds fly away from the canopy.

EXT.—BOBBY JOBBY DRIVING TO OURHOUSE

Robert Jobson (Bobby Jobby) the family's handyman and gardener is driving in his van along a country lane. He is on his way to Ourhouse to begin the week's work. The car stereo is playing soft acid-house music at a low volume. Bobby is mumbling the chorus of 'Driving Home for Xmas' by Chris Rea in an unsynchronised and gravelly voice over the top.

BOBBY JOBBY
Driving home for Christmas.

INT.—FAXON'S BEDROOM & WINDOW
FAXON'S MORNING SONG
BOBBY DROPS IN ON NEIGHBOURS
EXT.—GATE & DRIVE

Bobby Jobby arrives in his van at Ourhouse. He is met at the gate by Babydoll Wilson who helps him carry some bags from the van towards the house.

INT.—GREENHOUSE

Babydoll & Bobby Jobby sit together in the greenhouse. Babydoll is raised up on a throne-like chair and is wearing a clean, white ski-suit. Bobby sits in his regular work clothes. There are a number of small conicular piles of earth and mud in between them, also a teapot and some tea-cups bearing water and mud.

CUT BETWEEN WIDE AND MEDIUM SHOTS OF BOBBY AND BABYDOLL FILMED FROM OUTSIDE THROUGH THE GLASS AND

CLOSE UPS FILMED INSIDE.

BABYDOLL
Spell your name please.

Bobby Jobby begins to phonetically read out and write his name in the mud.

BOBBY JOBBY
Rob-ert-Job-son.

BABYDOLL
That's not your name.

BOBBY JOBBY
It is Babydoll. Robert Jobson is my name.

She crosses out his writing with a larger stick

BABYDOLL
Wrong. Your name is Jobby. Bobby
Jobby. I've got a new name for you.

Jobberts. But first, you must spell
the word 'CANT'.

BOBBY JOBBY
C-A-I-N-T. Caint.

Babydoll rises from her throne as she speaks and up-ends a small plant-pot of earth onto Bobby's head. She carefully shapes it into a conicular pile.

BABYDOLL
Coint? Incorrect. Cant. You can't
spell cant.

She finishes patting down the cone of earth on his head.

BABYDOLL
Stay still, stay still! There. Bless
you, Soilson. Now, is it a good loam?
(pointing at his face)
Think about it.

BOBBY JOBBY
(resigned)
Yes. It feels like it could well be a
decent loam.

BABYDOLL
Jardinière, how can you tell a loam
from the sky?

BOBBY JOBBY
(thinking)
The loam would stay on my head.

BABYDOLL
The sky would fly away!

BOBBY JOBBY
The lillies would prefer the loam.

BABYDOLL
Animals?

BOBBY JOBBY
Badgers. A loam's very popular with
a badger.

BABYDOLL
(delighted)
The badgers love a loam!

(becoming serious)
Now spell it.

BOBBY JOBBY
Spell what?

BABYDOLL
It. Pye. Wack. It. Spell Pyewacket.
Wait! I will make us a magic spell first,
for good energy.

She pours water onto one of the piles of earth and pats it down. She points to a potato.

BABYDOLL
What's that Bobby? What do you see there?

BOBBY JOBBY
Potato.
BABYDOLL
Pick up the potato.

BOBBY JOBBY
Don't want to.

BABYDOLL
Pick up the potato.

He picks the potato up.

BABYDOLL (CONT.)
What is it?

BOBBY JOBBY
A potato.

BABYDOLL
(aping him)
Tay-tuh! Tay-tuh. Bobby, Bobby! Put the taytuh in the earth and we can grow a po-tay-tuh tree!

He places the potato on top of the mound. She tips water from the teapot on top.

BOBBY JOBBY
Potatoes don't grow up into trees Missy. They grow down into the ground.

CUT TO:
EXT.—TREE CANOPY

Truson floats through the tree-tops, wobbling and balancing himself with exaggerated arm movements as he progresses from upper branch to branch. He attempts to scan the trees for wildlife with his binoculars as he moves. Birds and animals flee. Truson is perplexed by the lack of wildlife.

TRUSON
(to the tree tops)
Brother Thrush? Where are you brother Thrush?

CUT TO:
INT.—GREENHOUSE

BABYDOLL
Those are upside-down trees Bobby.
Don't you know that, Garden-Dunce?

BOBBY JOBBY
Shall we do the learning part now
Miss Anna?

BABYDOLL
(manipulating his cheeks)
Firstly, Wobbley Bobbley, firstly you
must learn to speak properly. You said
Cant and Pyewacket WRONGLY. Now! Try
and say it again correctly.

BOBBY JOBBY
*(exaggeratedly unhappily and
deliberately wrongly)*
Poy-warck-et

BABYDOLL
(aping him)
Pay-work-et.
(delighted)
Poy-wock-et! Good! Now say 'potato'!

BOBBY JOBBY
*(again deliberately
mispronouncing)*
Potato. Potato.

As he speaks she tips water into the cone of earth on his head. Muddy water dribbles down his face.

BOBBY JOBBY (CONT.)
(repeats)
Potato. Potato.

She pokes him in the cheeks, smearing the mud.

BABYDOLL
(delighted)
Earthman Pur-ter-turrr. Pur-tay-ter! Good! You have earned your new name, Bobby Purtayter. And the Pretty Purtayter Lady is your best wife. Can you say it with my finger in your globby?

She pushes her finger into his mouth.

BOBBY JOBBY
Pretty...purtayter....lay...

She moves around to whisper into his ear.

BABYDOLL
Sssshhh! The magic is working Bobby. Now.
(Solemn pause.)
It looks like you've got mufferts on your face!

BOBBY JOBBY
Mofferts?

BABYDOLL
Mufferts! I said Muff-uhrts! Do you know what Daddy says mufferts is?

CLOSE UP OFBOBBY'S FACE LOOKING CONCERNED

BABYDOLL (CONT.)
Special shaped sculptures!

BOBBY JOBBY
(sternly)
Missy! Don't be rude now.

BABYDOLL
He says it's a picture of your jimmy
licks!

BOBBY JOBBY
(laughing with her)
Now Miss. Annalise, will you stop with
that now?

BABYDOLL
Keep playing! I say 'Pyewacket' and
you write it in the ground

BOBBY JOBBY
Poy wacker urt

Bobby begins to make a line in the earth with his forefinger. Babydoll is spelling out 'Pyewacket' in the air with her own finger, gets half way through the word and then brings her finger to her face contemplatively. She sniffs it inquisitively and is repelled by its smell.

BABYDOLL
Uuurghhh! Bobby Jobby! Your willocky
smells awful. And you've not spelt one
word right yet.

A blurry figure passes over the greenhouse roof, bumping the glass with something it is carrying. We see this from Babydoll and Bobby's P.O.V.—the image is largely obscured by the glass, they glance up without really looking at him.

BABYDOLL
(waving up at Truson)
Morning Truson!

BOBBY JOBBY
(waving up at Truson)
Morning Truson!

NOTE:
Truson's voice is enthusiastic but muffled behind the glass as he passes.

TRUSON
Morning Babydoll! Morning Bobby!

BABYDOLL
Don't you ever want to learn to spell?
(walking around him, poking him)
You can't hear because you ears are
all hairy. I'll call you a silly sod!

NOTE:
Earth-related swear words ('sod', 'clot') are the worst for Bobby.

BOBBY JOBBY
(suddenly very angry)
Babydoll! Don't you use that word!

Babydoll looks taken aback, followed by a flash of anger.

CUT TO:
EXT.—LETTERBOX AT PERIMETER

Truson lands near the edge of the property. He pulls a plastic bag from his pocket and begins scouting around the bushes, furtling in the undergrowth. He retrieves a 12″ vinyl LP of free-jazz, addressed with a post-it note to "Faxon-Jackson Maddox-Wilson, Ourhouse, Europe" and places it into his bag. Turning around he reaches into another piece of foliage and retrieves a weighty, bubble-wrapped lumpen item, addressed with a post-it note to "Truson Maddox-Wilson, Ourhouse, Europe." He unwraps this package and uncovers a wooden facsimile of a prehistoric sculpture—the 'Venus of Hohle Fels'. Delighted, he holds it up to the morning sun. Just as he is about to leave he notices something deep inside the hedge. He crouches and reaches into it at full-stretch, retrieving a damp, crumpled letter in an envelope franked 'Council Services' and addressed to "Charles Maddox-Wilson, Ourhouse, Europe." It appears to be a few months old. He sniffs it.

TRUSON
Mildew.

Truson looks perturbed, pockets the letter and sets off back to the house on foot.

CUT TO:
INT.—GREENHOUSE

Babydoll is tipping more water into the cone of earth on Bobby's head. Mud is running down his face and he is holding a small potato between his teeth. She pushes the potato into his mouth and caps it with some earth.

BABYDOLL
Can you spell it if I wallops you?
Will that help you, Bobble? If I
wallop you in the face?
(shouting loudly)
Now say 'Mouth'!

BOBBY JOBBY
*(Abjectly through blocked
mouth whilst writing with
finger in the mud)*
Mowt

BABYDOLL
Naughty man!

Bobby finishes writing and looks down. We see that what he has actually written reads 'Breakfast!', Bobby spits out the potato and speaks clearly:

BOBBY JOBBY
Mouth. Now. Breakfast time Miss Anna.

BABYDOLL
Play! Play!

BOBBY JOBBY
No Missy, it's breakfast time now.

She tries to push more earth into his mouth.

BABYDOLL
Making breakfast! Making breakfast!

BOBBY JOBBY
(partly blocked mouth)

Breakfast time.

He spits out the remaining earth.

BABYDOLL
Urgghhh! You are disgusting.

BOBBY JOBBY
Thank you very much Miss Anna. I've got to go to work now.

He gets up.

BABYDOLL
He likes it! He likes it!

She kisses him on the cheek

BABYDOLL (CONT.)
(suddenly in a serious tone)
Thank me Jobby.

BOBBY JOBBY
Yes, thank you Babydoll and

In a quieter voice, talking to the tea cups and to the earth

BOBBY JOBBY (CONT.)
Thank you earth and thank you ground

Bobby walks off out of the greenhouse

BABYDOLL
He likes it.

FADE OUT

INT.—FAXON'S ROOM
INT.—KITCHEN
INT.—GROUND FLOOR OF HOUSE; ROOMS AND CORRIDORS

Truson and Faxon are walking together through the house looking for Daddy. Truson is holding the letter from the council.

TRUSON
(passing letter to Faxon)
Can you hold this for me? I've got something new that I'm so excited to show you, and I completely forgot to show you because of the effect of the jazz on me.

Faxon takes the letter, slightly reluctantly.

FAXON
I'm not sure that Daddy really likes it.

TRUSON
The letter or the music?

FAXON
Well, I meant the music, but—

TRUSON
(interrupting him)
Oh Daddy loves your music!

FAXON
Right, but what I meant to say was about...

Truson pulls the wrapped 'Venus' sculpture from his back-pack and again interrupts Faxon

TRUSON
Look, what I wanted to show you—I've
got this sculpture. Well, it's more
than that, really it's..

Unwrapping the sculpture

TRUSON (CONT.)
It's

FAXON
—got massive tits.

TRUSON
Faxon! Shhh.

FAXON
Quite a large fanny

TRUSON
(slightly shocked and embarrassed)
Actually it's really very interesting
that you say that, Faxon. Because
quite a lot of people think

Faxon reaches out to hold it and turns it over in his hand.

FAXON
(interrupting)
Look! The arse and fanny are the same thing. It's got an
arse-fanny. And big mammies. But really this sculpture
is all about the vagina, Truson.
It's a whopper.

TRUSON
(enthusiastically)
Yes, yes! That's right—because some people think she could—that it could be ancient pornology! Or a fertility Goddess.

FAXON
(laughing)
Pornology! Where's it from?

Truson does not understand Faxon's laughter.

TRUSON
Well, it's from Germany!

Truson cheerfully shows the stamps on the packaging to Faxon.

FAXON
How did you get it?

TRUSON
I ordered it on the line—you know—you let me use the...

FAXON
(interrupting)
Internet. I let you use the Internet and you ordered porn from Germany. Ha! Truson—don't tell Daddy I let you use the internet.

He pretends to strike out at the house with the sculpture.

FAXON (CONT.)
Maybe it's a weapon!

TRUSON
(distressed)
Faxon! Careful! This pornology is 35,000 years old!

Faxon stops gesturing and holds the sculpture in front of Truson.

FAXON
It looks a bit crusty.

TRUSON
Yes, because it's from the Cro-Magnon period. This is an artwork made by the very first humans. So don't break it! It's the first artwork by the first people!

FAXON
And—is that what they looked like?

TRUSON
Yes!

FAXON
With tiny heads and massive cockles?

TRUSON
Yes!

FAXON
And were they only 6 inches high?

TRUSON
Yes!

FAXON
It is an amazing thing. It's beautiful, like you. How do you know it's not fake?

Truson pauses, thinking.

TRUSON
What's a fake?

FAXON
Well, you know. Something that's not what it appears to be.

TRUSON
(laughing)
That's impossible!

FAXON
Wha?

TRUSON
Because look—

He takes the sculpture and holds it up in front of them.

TRUSON (CONT.)
It's right here.

CUT TO:
INT.—THE PUB
INT.—THE SWIMMING POOL
FADE IN:

Underwater shot, side view of Charles 'Daddy' Maddox-Wilson crouched in a foetal position. His long grey-black hair is billowing out freely in the water. His feet are pushed under a pair of nylon straps which are attached by suction-cups to the tiled floor of the swimming pool. These prevent Daddy from floating to the surface. He can step in and out of them as he wishes. He is holding a waterproof stop-watch in his right hand, and looking at it intently through the goggles. He appears to be shouting at it.

NOTE: ALL UNDERWATER SHOTS ACCOMPANIED BY MUFFLED FREE JAZZ OR KRAUTROCK, AS IF THE MUSIC WERE PIPED TO UNDERWATER SPEAKERS.

Daddy bursts to the surface of the pool, in the middle. He turns to find he is facing his two sons who have walked into the room.

DADDY
Hello boys.

TRUSON
Hello Daddy.

FAXON
Hello Dad.

DADDY
I feel incredibly upbeat today! Are
you feeling happy today? What have you
two been up to?

TRUSON
Daddy, I've been doing some
birdwatching in the trees again!

DADDY
Splendid! And Faxon, did your music
arrive?

FAXON
Yes, the free-jazz LP, the rare one.

Daddy walks into the shallow waters towards his sons.

DADDY
I was thinking about that. Why
shouldn't jazz be recorded in the
forest? Perhaps it all should! Why not
—after all—what is an instrument?

DADDY (CONT.)
When you think about it an instrument
is a tool—it has no fixed-form
besides that which..

TRUSON
(interrupting)
Daddy, I saw a starling today.

Daddy turns back and walks away into the deeper waters as he responds to Truson.

DADDY
Did you get a picture of it?

TRUSON
No I was—I was just enjoying looking
at it. And the birds. In the morning.

Daddy turns to face Truson.

DADDY
Truson. Consider this—of what use is
an experience if it goes unrecorded?

Truson looks confused.

DADDY (CONT.)
No use. It is of no use whatsoever. Undocumented experience is life thrown down the lavatory. It is worthless. Now Truson, I have an excellent digital camera and tripod which I am not using presently. These items are stored in the outhouse. Please take it and document the things you see! Make a portfolio. A collection of images, indeed of any images—is something we can talk about. And when all is said and done, perhaps, if you pursue this valiantly you may even be able to go back to university.

While he speaks Daddy is preoccupied with re-hooking himself to the floor of the pool

TRUSON
(excited)
Do you think I would be able to? Thank you! Thank you Daddy—I'd love to be able to make photographs of the things I see. One thing though—the starling made a funny sound—I think it said something to me—in my own voice. Shall I record that too, or are pictures better?

DADDY
(exasperated, shouts)
Time me!

Daddy plunges back beneath the surface clutching his stop watch and crouches on the floor of the pool. He starts the stop watch.

UNDERWATER SHOT OF HIS FACE, CHEEKS PUFFED-OUT, EYES INTENSELY STUDYING THE DIGITS. CUT TO DIGITS AND BACK TO HIS FACE. THIS CONTINUES AS THE STOP WATCH COUNTS UP TO A MINUTE.

FAXON

I think you'd better give him the letter.

TRUSON

(cheerfully)

Oh yes!

Truson steps forward to the middle-edge of the pool closest to Daddy's position and calls down towards the water.

TRUSON (CONT.)

Daddy!

Truson pats the surface of the water and talks to it.

TRUSON (CONT.)

Daddy!? Something came for you.

Daddy leaps upwards from the pool-floor to the surface and raises his arms in Truson's direction.

DADDY

(gasping for air)

Truson! When will you learn the value
of concentration? Reclaim your brain!

Truson produces the crumpled letter and proffers it to Daddy.

TRUSON

Daddy this letter came for you.

DADDY

Letter? A letter in an envelope? Is it franked?

TRUSON

It says "Council Services"

DADDY

Give it to me!

Truson is stuck as he can't get any closer to Daddy without entering the pool and Daddy is not moving from the middle of the water. Truson looks perplexed. Daddy is becoming irritable.

DADDY (CONT.)

Pass it here boy. Throw it over!

Truson raises the letter up with his right hand and throws it upwards with a flick of the wrist. The letter rotates in a parabola heading towards Daddy in the middle of the pool.

FAXON

Oh that's a good throw!

Daddy looks shocked and shields himself as if anticipating a blow from a heavy object. The letter alights on the surface of the water in front of his cowering figure. Truson and Faxon glance at each other in concern. Daddy gathers himself, steps forward and plucks the envelope from the surface of the water. He opens it and extracts two pieces of A4 paper in duplicate—pink & white. These are formally addressed to him but feature strange ciphers. Daddy becomes agitated. As he talks Truson drifts and becomes preoccupied with his Venus of Hohle Fels replica.

DADDY
Boys! I will say only this—this nation is in administration. And Bureaucracy is pub-lic enemy num-ber one. But I, Charlie Wilson will not be dictated to by these fucking management drones! They are...Truson! What is that?

TRUSON
It's a Venus!

DADDY
And where did you get it from?

TRUSON
Germany. I got it on E-bay Daddy!

FAXON
On the internet—I let him use my..

DADDY
Faxon! I allowed you to have that internet in good faith, for cultural reasons.And now your brother is woofing up four-flushing museum pieces from German entrepeneurs. Please make sure this does not happen again—or I shall turn the internet off. Do you understand?

FAXON
Yes Daddy.

DADDY
And for God's sake use the cables.
I won't have books and pictures flying
through the air unchecked.

TRUSON
Yes Daddy!

FAXON
Yes Daddy.

DADDY
(turning away, and talking to the pool)
Why do people want to be all joined up
anyway? We'll all become the same.
For example, an internet connection
on a plane that's crashing would
enable the passengers to solicit a
refund. Now that can't be good for the
airline companies, is it?

FAXON
No Daddy.

DADDY
(turning back to his sons, more focused)
Good. Now then. Where was I? Ah yes—
These bloody councillors—want things
from me. I will fight them on my own
beach and in my own garden if
necessary. And I will read this
underwater!
(shouts)
Time me!

Daddy plunges underwater clutching the 2 pages of the letter.

The muffled music continues.

Daddy is crouching on the floor of the pool again, holding the letter in front of him. He is shouting angrily at it. It becomes illegible before it turns to mulch.

EXT.—THE GARDEN

Bobby is working in the garden near to the house. Daddy, in skinny jeans and unbuttoned shirt, still partly wet from the pool,towelling himself, walks around the outside of the house and is passing Bobby.

BOBBY JOBBY
I gave the neighbours your pie.

DADDY
(pleased with himself)
And, how did that go down? Were they—placated?

BOBBY JOBBY
He seemed unhappy with it. And a bit confused.

DADDY
Confusion eh? Poor fellow. We must clarify the situation. Bobby, order a huge pie from the baker in the village. Ask him for the largest pie he can fabricate. And deliver this pie to The Crusts tomorrow.

BOBBY JOBBY
Mr Wilson is it wise to wind them up? He said to say they are monitoring the situation. Will you be going round there?

DADDY
There? There? Can't can't can't. I am too busy working here.

Daddy strides off.

DADDY (CONT.)
(gesturing as he walks away)
More pie!

INT.—THE THEATRE

In a sparse theatre back-room Daddy is sitting on a backwards chair with his arms resting on the chair's back-support. He is meeting with 3 actors and a director—Brian Wurgan. Daddy is hiring this ensemble to be his latest in-house theatre group. He is attempting to introduce his concept of a spontaneous form of theatre derived from everyday situations. This is the project Daddy has hired them in to work on. Brian, the 'director', is struggling to understand the difference between reality and theatre in Daddy's formulation. The actors, at least for now, are happy to say 'yes' to Daddy, and secure the job.

BRIAN
So Mr. Wilson , what is my role here, precisely?

DADDY
You're the director.

BRIAN
And you are?

DADDY
I'm the director-director.

BRIAN
The director-director?

DADDY
Oui. You direct the play. I direct you, directing the play.

BRIAN
Why don't you just direct the play?

DADDY
I am directing the play. Through the medium of you.

BRIAN
The medium of me?

DADDY
Yes Brian. You play the director.

ACTOR*1
Oh right, I get it.

Brian, the director, does not get it.

DADDY
Do you "get it" Brian?

BRIAN
Yes.

DADDY
Everyone, 'listen up', I will explain this just the once. I imagine an original play every single day.
(Pause)

DADDY (CONT.)
You realise the play.
(Pause)

DADDY (CONT.)
There.

ACTOR*2
Terrific!

ACTOR*3
Super!

Brian, the director, scowls at the actors, who he believes are being obsequious.

BRIAN
But why don't you direct, why use..

DADDY
I am directing it. Look Brian, every day very real, very fleeting things happen. Right?

BRIAN
Yes?

DADDY
Great.
(Pause)

DADDY (CONT.)
Now, this structure is called "Play A Day."

ACTOR*3
Oh, good title!

DADDY
Thank you.

BRIAN
Sorry—"Very real things happen"? And?

DADDY
Things with a poignancy and er, a flavour which are lacking in more conventional theatre. I channel these things and I harvest them. I lay them out to dry. Like corn, or Spanish ham. However Brian
(beginning to shout)

DADDY (CONT.)
if you do not wish to dine with us I can call my agent to call a car to take you outside!

ACTOR *1
(cutting in to retrieve the situation)
Really Mr. Wilson I can assure you we are delighted to be your guests.

BRIAN
Delighted to be working with you on your new material.

DADDY
Brian, do I resemble a haberdasher or a dress-maker?

BRIAN
Look—I'm sorry—I just want to establish some roles—rules that will enable the group to work.

DADDY
Brian. I believe you are a very good director.This is why you must workshop this group constantly, in order to be ready when I make my deposit! We are aiming for something highly concentrated. I will imagine an idea for a play, every day, directly from reality. You must feel absolute freedom to interpret this work in any way that you see fit, experimentally. Because you play the role of the director! Voila!

INT—DISTURBING PHONECALL *1

There are several phones, in a range of styles, throughout the house. They all ring.
SFX: Phones ringing, multiple ring-tones.

Truson is near to one and picks it up.

TRUSON
Hello.

Truson hears a strange voice through the receiver; it sounds like a mixture of machine code and someone talking with a voice box through a pitch-shifter.

VOICE FROM PHONE
Badasdbjhbdfwanadmnasd.

TRUSON
I've got a bad line. Hello? This is Truson Wilson-Maddox speaking. Who's that?

VOICE FROM PHONE
Prhwsjfsbsdmnfsmnahjsdgjaahhh!

TRUSON
(anxious)
Crikey! Would you like to speak with someone's voice?

VOICE FROM PHONE
Yuerwyifsddghhghthththth!

TRUSON
They're not here right now. Can you call back? Please can you call back later?

Truson hangs up the phone, looking worried.

CUT TO:
EXT.—TRUSON FINDS DADDY IN THE GARDEN

Daddy is crouching by a fence in the garden, peering into a detached double-glazed window that is covered in snails.

DADDY
Now this could work as a means of exchange between the inside and the outside, figuratively.

Truson approaches him, slightly tentatively.

DADDY
Truson I'm working!

TRUSON
Sorry Daddy it's just that there was a phone call with a strange voice. It sounded like a robot talking to me. What should we do?

DADDY
Truson I am working. Use your initiative. Tell them to call back.

TRUSON
(pleased)
I did!

DADDY
(bored)
In that case—answerphone. Set up the answerphone. It's in the pantry—set it up in the lounge on the first phone on the ground floor, and then we shan't be disrupted by cold-callers.

TRUSON
Daddy. What do you think it was?

DADDY
(shooing him away)
Truson pshhhh! Go and fix it up, there's a good lad! I am trying to write.

Daddy returns to his contemplation of the window.

EXT.—BOBBY'S VAN

Bobby whistles and jingles his car keys as he strolls around the outside of the building. He turns to find his van has been graffiti-ed with excrement; the words "Bobby Jobby CANT" cover the top half of one side of the van.

BOBBY JOBBY
Oh what's she gone and done that for, for goodness sake?

Truson appears on his way back to the house.

TRUSON
Bobby! What's happened?

BOBBY JOBBY
Bobby Jobby coynt.

TRUSON
That's a song.

BOBBY JOBBY
Eh?

TRUSON
A 'cant' is a song, it's Latin, I remember that from school.

BOBBY JOBBY
Sure, it's Irish for speech too.
But I don't...

TRUSON
(interrupting)
How lovely! Shall we sing a song
together Bobby?

BOBBY JOBBY
No Truson, I'm not in the mood. I need
to speak to Miss Anna about this. I'm
not happy about this at all. She's
ruined me van.

TRUSON
How do you know it was her?

BOBBY JOBBY
She had me spelling that word this
morning when we were playing.

TRUSON
Then I'm sure it's only a game Bobby.

BOBBY JOBBY
(with air of resignation)
Sure she thinks it's a game.
I'll get it.

INT.—GALLERY OPENING

Daddy and Babydoll are in an art gallery inside the house. They are standing next to a small table bearing wine glasses full of a crisp, chilled white wine and several bottles are lined up, as if in anticipation of visitors. Daddy and Babydoll are the only people in the room.

The room also features a sculpture by Babydoll—a potato attached to a small portable tape machine by a series of straws and coloured pieces of string, mounted on a pile of lego held together with sellotape. The tape machine is periodically emitting moaning sounds, as if it were in pain. On one of the walls a cotton bud sticks out horizontally from a lump of blu-tack at about waist height.

Babydoll has changed outfit and is dressed rather glamourously. Daddy's outfit is the same apart from being cleaned and ironed.

CLOSE UP OF WINE GLASSES CHINKING TOGETHER IN FRONT OF TABLE FULL OF WINE.

DADDY (V.O.)
Cheers!

BABYDOLL (V.O.)
Cheers!

DADDY
I'm not late am I?

BABYDOLL
No.

DADDY
Well done you!

DADDY (V.O.)
Cheers!
BABYDOLL (V.O.)
Cheers!

DADDY
I'm not late am I?

BABYDOLL
No.

DADDY
Well done you!

BABYDOLL
Thank you Daddy.

They drink the white wine.

DADDY
So, what were you thinking about,
with this one?

CLOSE UP OF THE ARRANGEMENT OF THE POTATO, STRING, LEGO AND SELLOTAPE.

BABYDOLL
I was thinking about a kind of a
constellation.

DADDY
A, erm... cluster?

BABYDOLL
A clustering yes—a structure, which
is evanescent, in a sense. An
assemblage as a kind of furgacious
energy system.

DADDY
So the potato...

BABYDOLL
The rhizome is a kind of battery. But it's not just formal, I was thinking—hoping to invoke a kind of social propinquity...

The tape machine emits a moaning noise.

DADDY
I think that comes across terribly well.

He reaches out to touch her arm, hoping for some physical reciprocation, receiving none.

BABYDOLL
Thank you Daddy. What else do you think?

He struggles a little bit, walks around the space. The tape continues to moan. He spots the Q-Tip and makes a bee-line for it!

DADDY
Hmmmmmm. Hmmmmmmm. This, this!
(pointing)
I absolutely love this. It makes it!
What were you thinking with this?

BABYDOLL
Broadcasting. It's—broadcasting.

CLOSE UP OF THE Q-TIP STICKING OUT OF THE WALL.

DADDY (V.O.)
Genius.

DADDY
I think that comes across terribly well.

He reaches out to touch her arm, hoping for some physical reciprocation, receiving none.

BABYDOLL
Thank you Daddy. What else do you think?

He struggles a little bit, walks around the space. The tape continues to moan. He spots the Q-Tip and makes a bee-line for it!

DADDY
Hmmmmmm. Hmmmmmmm. This, this!
(pointing)
I absolutely love this. It makes it! What were you thinking with this?

BABYDOLL
It's—broadcasting. That part is broadcasting.

CLOSE UP OF THE Q-TIP STICKING OUT OF THE WALL.

DADDY (V.O.)
Genius.

INT.—TRUSON DISCOVERSTHE OBJECT

Truson is heading towards the living room carrying an old answerphone system. He is struggling to organise its lengthy cabling as he walks down the corridor towards the living room. He becomes tangled and stops walking for a moment to concentrate on trying to find the end of the cable. Further down the corridor, in the living room, the phone rings. Truson is startled; he becomes more tangled.

TRUSON
Oh monkeys! Coming!

Truson enters the room. He does not react to the inhabiting Object. He does not appear to notice it. Instead he walks straight up to the ringing phone and looks to find a way to plug in the tangled answerphone. He picks up the ringing phone set, looking for some kind of socket. This causes its receiver to fall. He catches the receiver, inadvertently answering the call he sought to avoid. He feels compelled to speak.

TRUSON
Hello? Yes, it's Truson Wilson-Maddox.
Sis.? Well, no, but I haven't heard
from you forever! Family? Yes, Daddy.
He's working. Of course, I can get him
for you, I can...no it's fine...I'll just...

Truson turns around. He is standing directly facing The Object from about 12 feet. Suddenly, as if a switch were flipped, his awareness of The Object is activated. He can see something alien in the room. He drops the phone. It is tangled with the answerphone and bounces and dangles on its cable. Truson opens his mouth and eyes wide in terror then unleashes a tremendous and continuous scream which rattles through the house.

TRUSON
Argghhhhhhh!

We see what various members of Ourhouse are doing at the moment of Truson's scream:

CUT TO:
INT.—FAXON'S BEDROOM

Faxon in his room mixing some music. The scream begins, Faxon looks concerned, turns off his amplifier and sets off in the direction of the sound.

CUT TO:
EXT.—DADDY IN THE GARDEN

Daddy is circling in the garden, thinking and chuntering to himself. He is disturbed by the sound. He attempts to bat it away, but it continues. He strides off in the direction of the house to determine the source of the annoying sound.

CUT TO:
INT.—BABYDOLL'S ART STUDIO

Babydoll, in her studio, working at a desk gluing drinking straws into a potato next to an arrangement of Lego. Babydoll is in 'work' mode—she is wearing designer spectacles and overalls. The scream begins and she flinches, looking concerned.

BABYDOLL
Truson.

Adopting an air of responsibility and concern she puts down her work, pushes her glasses up onto her face and stands up to go downstairs.

CUT TO:
EXT.—THE DRIVE

Bobby Jobby, about to begin cleaning up his van with soapy water, hears the sound and puts his sponge down.

CUT TO:
INT.—THE PUB

Uncle Tommy sitting in the pub, smoking a cigarette and drinking a G & T. The jukebox plays. The scream begins. Tommy pricks up his ears then raises his index finger in the air as if to say 'one moment'. He downs his drink, stubs out his cigarette and rises. He turns and walks straight to the bar.

TOMMY
One more G.& T. please love.

CUT TO:
INT.—FRONT-ROOM FAMILY ENCOUNTERTHE OBJECT 1

Close up of Truson's screaming face. The scream ends. Pull-back to reveal Faxon, Babydoll and Daddy looking into the room in dismay. They are staring at The Object.

BABYDOLL
What. Is. That.

FAXON
That is

DADDY
There

BABYDOLL
Where

DADDY
It

BABYDOLL
What

DADDY
Is.

TRUSON
Not. I can't see "is".

DADDY
There.
(triumphantly)
There! There it is! And I thought I'd
never see it again.

He steps forwards and walks past The Object. Stops and looks confused.

DADDY (CONT.)
Hang on a minute.

FAXON
Is it a skittle?

DADDY
No.

BABYDOLL
No.

FAXON
But falling down hole

TRUSON
I can't...

DADDY
(earnestly)
It's my Eames chair, and
(chuckling)
honestly kids—I thought I'd never
see it again!

Daddy turns and around in a squatting motion, lifts his lower jacket and slowly backs up towards The Object as if it is a stool that he is preparing to sit on. He misses the Object by about a metre and falls on his arse.

TRUSON
... see anything.

BABYDOLL
Oh poor sausage!

DADDY
(from the floor)
A hole! A hole! Call Mr. Jobson and
ask him to fix it up. Truson—it could be—
(he looks from Truson to The Object and back)
—you could be—a young space hole.
A temporal hourglass a good,
old fashioned

TRUSON
Reaper.

FAXON
Shhhh!

BABYDOLL
Don't make him secret

TRUSON
Reaper

DADDY
(clicks fingers)
Yes temporal, but chronological
and civil.

FAXON
Is it a skittle?

TRUSON
Sickle

BABYDOLL
Cipher!

DADDY
Cipher!

DADDY
No, really, I've seen this before.
It's one of my...it's one of mine.

He begins to back up to it again.

Uncle Tommy arrives and joins the group looking into the room.

BABYDOLL
No I don't think it's yours I think
it's from my.

FAXON
Sculpture?

BABYDOLL
That plastic and anaglyptical...wurst.

TOMMY
(shouting)
Twat pomade twat!

FAXON
Hello Uncle Tommy!

TRUSON
Hello Uncle Tommy!

Daddy falls over again near to The Object.

Tommy lights a cigarette and walks off.

DADDY
Delighted! Delighted to have you back.

FAXON
Always. Here.

TRUSON
A tree in Ourhouse. A tree.

BABYDOLL
Daddy I've seen this before, it's one of my—

TRUSON
(shouting)
It's very windy in here turn it off.

Bobby arrives.

DADDY
Bobby!

Charles Wilson, crouched near the figure and with his jacket tails raised gestures to Bobby as if to beckon him over. Bobby does not move.

BOBBY JOBBY
Oh dear.

Daddy continues to beckon Bobby, with a manic smile on his face.

DADDY
No old friend! Family! One of!

BOBBY JOBBY
(sighs)
We've got a problem here.
(Under his breath)
Driving home for Christmas.

FAXON
An old fashioned

BABYDOLL
Hourglass!

DADDY
Hourglass!

TRUSON
(weeping)
And reaper.

Daddy begins backing up to The Object again.

DADDY
Truson be explicit! I've seen this before, in my old shin-pad box. No, wrong! I dis-engraved. In my school play. I dreamt I was a school play!

TRUSON
Cast! Cut! Chisel! Hew!

BABYDOLL
Cast! Cut! Chisel! Hew!

FAXON
Cast! Cut! Chisel! Hew!

DADDY
The poor planets must rise. We must help them do their allotment.

Bobby Jobby leaves.

BABYDOLL
(acknowledging Bobby's exit)
It is windy in here.

TRUSON
(anxious, mechanical,smiling)
I can't hear it above 8 miles. Silent, and approximate point of feedback of less than one inch and above 300 megahurz. It is the sound of death, feeling, death, feeling, it's a frequency it has a bandwidth and we could make a radio station for it we could make dead radio if we weren't inside the mirror. If we could break

the composite we could make it. It
can't think outside the loop. Help me.

BABYDOLL
Stop out of the hourglass.

Truson steps towards the group, away from the Object.

TRUSON
(happily)
Oh biscuits and tea, the sounds gone!

Daddy falls on his arse again.

FAXON
This could take some time.

DADDY
Is it my old shin reaper? My wild
willy car toad?

TRUSON
I can't see anything. The rays are
coming out of my eyes. Across the
thingies, and blinding them.

DADDY
Thingies!

BABYDOLL
Thingies!

FAXON
Thingies!

BABYDOLL
(to Daddy)
It is not your Thingy!

DADDY
(picking himself up, smiling)
It most certainly will. It is my new aging familiar.

Uncle Tommy re-joins the group, holding a glass of scotch.

TRUSON
Congratulations from incomplete data—it's our Thingy at least we can say that for us together can't we?

UNCLE TOMMY
Hear hear! Now, if we can, lets leave the amazing thing alone. Which of you children would like to join Uncle Tommy for a nightcap before the warming hearth of the local pub? I have 50 pence, which I believe is enough for a round of drinks.

FAXON
Me!

TRUSON
Me!

Daddy falls on his arse again.

BABYDOLL
Me!

DADDY
Me!

END OF EPISODE ONE

"EPISODE 2—CLASS"

INT.—KITCHEN, NIGHT TIME

Bobby Jobby is snoozing in a chair in the kitchen. He is holding a silicon dispenser which has leaked onto his jeans.

CUT TO:
INT.—CORRIDOR BY LIVING-ROOM

SFX: paper being torn and scrunched up accompanied by grunting, troughing and heavy nasal breathing, like an animal feeding, greedily .

CUT TO:
INT.—KITCHEN, NIGHT TIME

Bobby Jobby stirs in his sleep.

CUT TO:
INT.—CORRIDOR BY LIVING-ROOM

SFX: A book falls to the floor in the lounge making a louder thudding noise over the ongoing sounds of paper-tearing and urgent feeding.

CUT TO:
INT.—KITCHEN, NIGHT TIME

Bobby Jobby is awake. He registers the strange sounds emanating from the living-room down the corridor. Bobby assumes it must be some kind of animal that has gotten stuck in the house, or a rat. He resolves to go and free it. Moving to stand up he notices the silicon dispenser and glue in his lap, which he accidentally transfers to his hands as he moves the dispenser onto the table.

BOBBY JOBBY
Grout. Psshhh.

Bobby reaches for some tissues which get stuck to the glue on his fingers. He reaches for more tissues which also adhere, compounding the problem. He temporarily gives up on cleaning his hands and picks up a broom. He walks down the corridor and turns into the entrance to the living room. The door is open, Bobby stands in the doorway facing into the room. Bobby's eyes open wide in horror. His jaw drops. He releases the broom, which falls a few inches and dangles above the floor, prevented from falling completely to the floor by a strand of silicon glue.

BOBBY JOBBY
Jesus!

CUT TO:THE OBJECT, STANDING 4 METRES FROM BOBBY IN THE MIDDLE OF THE ROOM.

The Object is staring directly at Bobby. It is also holding a book open with one hand in front of its chest and chewing something. It swallows and burps. The book it is holding is "The Classic Slum: Salford Life in the First Quarter of the Century" by Robert Roberts. Without breaking eye contact with Bobby The Object tears a page from the book, crumples it into a ball using only one hand and pushes the ball of paper into its own mouth. It begins to chew again. The action of mastication is exaggerated and noisy and appears to be directed at Bobby. The Object does not move from the spot it is occupying. Bobby slowly reaches down to the broom with his left hand and extends it outwards from himself towards the open door, hooking it and pulling it towards him. As it closes in Bobby reaches out with his right hand—which still has tissues stuck to it—and, with a sharp movement, grabs the door-knob and pulls the door shut in front of his own face.

BOBBY JOBBY
(relieved)
Christ.

INT.—DADDY'S BEDROOM, MORNING

Daddy is dressing in his bedroom next to the sleeping Babydoll. He appears to be in a chipper mood and is whistling like a milkman. He is wearing his normal skinny jeans and black silk shirt. Going to select footwear he finds an incongruous pair of futuristic trainers sited within his normal footwear line up.

DADDY
Ah!

Daddy reaches down and selects the trainers.

CUT TO:
INT.—DADDY'S BATHROOM

There is a similarly incongruous gold bracelet on Daddy's sink.

DADDY
Ah!

Daddy reaches down and picks up the bracelet and puts it on.

CUT TO:

Daddy is attempting to style his permanently unstyled hair using a lot of hair-gel and a comb. He constructs a strange bouffant with side-parting. He appears pleased with it.

DADDY
(cheerfully)
Don't be a spanner!
(singing to himself, quietly)
M.C. Hammer.

He picks up a pair of Oakley sunglasses from a dresser and puts them on. These affectations—the shades, bracelet, trainers and hair—clash blatantly with the rest of his clothes. In this episode, under the influence of The Object, Daddy believes he is working class. He strides cheerfully out of the bedroom.

INT.—THE LIVING ROOM

The Object's has one arm outstretched and its mouth is opening and closing, like a fish.

Daddy walks down the adjoining corridor, whistling cheerfully. He swings into the living room holding onto the door-frame and does a little jig—

DADDY
Morning mate!

—and swings back out again, continuing on his way to breakfast.

The Object's position and action continue; its mouth opening and closing.

Faxon enters the room reading the classifieds from a local paper. He folds the newspaper under his arm as he walks up to The Object. He stands directly facing the Object, but appears to be looking through it, as if he is seeing something else just behind it. Faxon reaches into his trouser pocket and digs around, producing a fifty pence piece.

FAXON
Heads!

He flips the coin from his right hand up in the air. It lands in The Object's opening and closing mouth. The Object does not react.

Faxon reaches back into his pocket, which is now empty.

FAXON (CONT.)
(disappointed)
That was my last 50 pence.

INT. KITCHEN—BREAKFAST

Faxon enters the kitchen and joins Daddy, Babydoll and Truson at the breakfast table. Daddy is wearing his Oakley shades.

DADDY
(enthused)
Alright mate!

FAXON
(grumpily)
Morning Daddy. I like your shades.

DADDY
Cheery-ta little chappy!

Although it is Daddy who is behaving strangely, Truson picks up on Faxon's downbeat air.

TRUSON
Faxon are you alright?

FAXON
No, I have lost all my money. I'm broke.

BABYDOLL
Lost it where?

FAXON
I don't know. Gambling, maybe?

DADDY
(confused)
Gambling?
(suddenly brightens)
Terrific! The me-me of luck runs through our family like a virus!
(Beaming)
Luck and madness.

TRUSON
(interrupting)
Daddy, what's a me-me?

DADDY
...erm, I dunno. Just a thing. Sunshine.

He puts a matchstick in his mouth.

DADDY (CONT.)
Don't worry about it Truson! Faxon! You have got no money? Absolutely No money? Are you sure?

FAXON
Yes Daddy.

DADDY
(very cheerfully)
Wonderful. Being poor is an acutely valuable experience which, when I was your age, I had to travel some distance to curry. You are a very fortunate young man—you can be poor locally. Now—there is a job going down the pub which you must take up

immediately, me Hearty. Go and see
Lorraine, the pub Landlady. Tell her I
sent you. Hoowahhh!

FAXON
Down the pub?

DADDY
Dahn the pub! Dahn the pub! The
British public house is a superb
place! Off you go Faxon! Go out there
and get a job.

Daddy chivvies him along with a clapping gesture. Faxon leaves the table rather unhappily and exits the room.

Babydoll, smiling, is contemplating the role-play options that Daddy's new downwardly mobile fantasy affords her. Truson, not following the conversation, is looking at something up near the ceiling that is interesting to him.

DADDY (CONT.)
(to Babydoll and the
inattentive Truson)
This puts me in mind of a blinding
idea. It's pure gold. I tell you what.
I intend to spend the entire day 'dahn
pub'. I will mix with the locals,
drink a few bevvies and write a play.
(to Babydoll)
Will you join me, lav?

Babydoll has produced her lipstick and compact and is, making herself up.

BABYDOLL
(beaming, with bright-red lips)
'Course, I'd fackin' love to Babe. I just 'ave to get changed, dunni? I'll meet yer dahn there.

INT.—THE PUB

A small pub interior. The pub is empty apart from Uncle Tommy who is encapsulated inside a portable television on the bar, and a group of workers in work-wear, apparently on a break, seated around a larger table in the background. This group is looking at black and white photographs, drinking beer, eating peanuts and chatting. These workers are employed by Daddy but never do any real work on the house. They are in fact a Trade Union re-enactment society masquerading as workmen whom Daddy has inadvertently employed. No-one is aware of this and it is never made explicit—it is only evidenced through their preoccupations inside the pub. They are never seen outside the pub.

The pub is inside the house. The viewer is not yet aware of this.

Faxon is working behind the bar, pulling a pint of lager for Uncle Tommy.

UNCLE TOMMY
And a chaser. Scotch please Faxon.

Uncle Tommy gives Faxon fifty pence. Everything inside Ourhouse costs 50 pence. The older, larger coin type.

UNCLE TOMMY
Nice to see you down here. Stick the tv on.

FAXON
It's a job I suppose.

Faxon presses a remote and turns on a large, cathode ray tube TV from the 90s. A premiership football match from the 90s is being shown.

UNCLE TOMMY
All footballers are rapists.

FAXON
How do you know that?

UNCLE TOMMY
I used to be one.

FAXON
Ha!
(pause)
Really?

UNCLE TOMMY
How's your brother?

FAXON
He's beautiful. He said that his sister called yesterday. Uncle Tommy, what's her name?

UNCLE TOMMY
He hasn't got a sister.

FAXON
He said she lives outside.

UNCLE TOMMY
(downing a can of Grolsch)
Nope.

DADDY (V.O.)
A pint of pub please!

Charles has arrived at the bar, in his new regalia—shades, bracelet, trainers—now additionally augmented with a bright orange 'Oregon Beavers' baseball cap and a pair of Zubaz body-builders pants. Daddy's t-shirt changes from scene to scene in the pub, working through a series of branded & self-consciously 'offensive' statements.

FAXON
(confused)
We've got beer and lager and crisps.

DADDY
Yes please!

FAXON
What would you like?

DADDY
Hmmm. I'll take a pint of Guinness—
in a yard glass.

UNCLE TOMMY
(scoffing)
Arf!

DADDY
And a packet of Mr. Porky's.

UNCLE TOMMY
Oh! Ha ha ha!

DADDY
(witheringly)
Shouldn't you be in the pub?

Faxon passes a half-pint of lager over the bar to Daddy, who looks pleased with it. He puts a 50 pence piece down on the bar.

FAXON
(pushing the note back to Daddy)
You don't have to pay Sir.

DADDY
(pushing the note back)
But I insist mate!

Faxon cashes the pound note and puts a large, old-fashioned 50 pence piece down on the bar as change.

UNCLE TOMMY
What's up with you today?

DADDY
Squat-all Matey. I am here today to
work on my new play. I will be here
all day. My bird will be joining me.

Tommy steals the 50 pence.

UNCLE TOMMY
(faking enthusiasm)
Great.

DADDY
The only man that can stop me is the tax-man, eh Tommy! Eh? The British pub! A creative hub! God bless. Cheers!

He takes a swig from his glass. Mid-gulp he checks himself, lowers the glass and raises his hand in the air.

DADDY (CONT.)
Now, before I forget meself—who would like a brew? Faxon—buy a round on the house!

FAXON
Eh?

DADDY
A round on the house please mate.

Daddy makes a patronising clapping gesture, as if to chivvy Faxon along.

DADDY (CONT.)
Buy everyone a drink pal!

UNCLE TOMMY
Brandy please Faxon.

DADDY
And I'll have a Stella on the rocks. Bring it over—I am about to work on my new play—

As he walks across towards a table he addresses the group of workers.

DADDY
Lads! What would you like?

They ignore him. He puts his arm round the shoulder of one of the workers, who continues to ignore him.

DADDY (CONT.)
Mate, you just order whatever, OK Pal?

Daddy takes up a seat next to a small table.

INT.—THE PUB
INT.—THE PUB, DADDY & BABYDOLL'S TABLE

DADDY
Goolies goolies goolies! I'm bovvered...about the director. He seems quite
(clenching his fist)
—closed. The actors are quite—sound. Money? Money could be a problem too. It's tight. Funding? Shit funding, babe!

BABYDOLL
I fought you were the fundin' babe?

DADDY
I am. But—I ain't got no groats ave I love?

Digging in his pockets, pulling out the lining.

DADDY
Look! I'm completely brazz-cocked. The
fucking tax-man is right on my case!
He's doing my nut. Lend us some money
darling—cash—just for the round.

Babydoll indulges him. She produces a 50 pence piece from her purse.

BABYDOLL
My poor ducky. Here you are dear.
Vodka-tonic please.

DADDY
Mental!

She gives him the 50 pence. Daddy goes to the bar.

INT.—THE PUB; DADDY AT BAR

Lorraine is pulling drinks for Daddy. Daddy's accent is oscillating within sentences, cracking back into R.P. at certain moments—under duress, or when trying to make an impression.

DADDY
So, like I was saying, I was at
University with Mick Jagger and then
at prep-school with Richard Branson.
I'm still pretty good mates with them.
Tony Blair was there too—he's a c**t
though. Can't play guitar.
Despite what happened, I am much
better than that wanker!

Lorraine is suitably unimpressed, she presents the drinks. Daddy gives her the 50 pence. And returns to his table.

LORRAINE
I wish you'd get out my bloody pub.

INT.—THE PUB, DADDY RETURNS TO TABLE

Daddy is carrying his yard glass and Babydoll's vodka and tonic through the pub to his table. He passes the workers' group and glances against a worker's out-stretched leg, slightly spilling the drinks. He is angered but takes the drinks to Babydoll before returning to confront the worker, who has his back to him.

DADDY
Oi Mate!

Daddy taps the worker on the back. The worker does not move. Daddy continues to tap him on the back.

DADDY (CONT.)
Excuse me. My drinks Pal. But also—

why are you not working? Why are my hedges still the same height? Why is the roof not undergoing repair? What am I employing you for? Why-are you not-doing-what-you-are-paid-to-do?

The worker does not turn or respond.

DADDY (CONT.)
(visibly angered)
Listen you louts, I will not suffer base insolence! Alright Pal!?

Daddy holds the worker by the arms and moves around him. When Daddy has managed to position himself between the worker and the table he begins slapping the worker in the face, repeatedly and hard.

DADDY (CONT.)
Work shit, work!

The worker looks blankly on, unaffected by Daddy's violence. Daddy becomes self-conscious about his loss of control.

DADDY (CONT.)
Ha!

He straightens the worker's coat.

DADDY (CONT.)
There we are. A lesson learnt.No bovver mate. It's no problem son. Carry on. I was only joking.

Babydoll is laughing as Daddy returns to his seat.
She stops laughing.

BABYDOLL
Charles, what are you doing?

INT.—THE PUB BAR

Truson is sitting at the bar, showing his Venus to Lorraine.

LORRAINE
That looks a bit fake.

Bobby Jobby approaches Truson at the bar and tries to explain that he has seen The Object eating a book during the night. Bobby is distressed and struggling to communicate, affiicted by the same aphasia effect that the group suffered when trying to talk about The Object the night before.

TRUSON
Hello Bobby!

BOBBY JOBBY
Truson. I saw a ...white dwarf...sucking in a star. No! Wrong night round events in sequence. There's a ghost-train. And I'm on the ghost-train.

TRUSON
Bobby. I-dont-understand-what-you-are trying-to-say.

Bobby mimes pulling a steam-whistle.

BOBBY JOBBY
Whoo! Whoo! The rush of air—creates blindness, blindness!
(to himself, with eyes shut)

BOBBY JOBBY (CONT.)
Driving home for Christmas.

UNCLE TOMMY
(slurring)
Get him a drink Lorraine. Scotch for young Robert. Clearly the boy's struggling, mentally.

TRUSON
What did you see Bobby?

BOBBY JOBBY
(still with eyes shut)
Bah. Bah.

TRUSON
Are you hurt?

BOBBY JOBBY
(opening eyes)
No I'm fine. I'm not hurt I just bah!

TRUSON
Lorraine, have you got any pens?

LORRAINE
Yeah I've got some down here as it goes.
You want a bit of paper and all?

UNCLE TOMMY
(slurring)
Leave it Truson, he's bleating.
Obviously in some—stupidity.

The landlady passes Truson a biro, an A4 pad of paper and a packet of felt-tips. Truson puts the paper and biro in front of Bobby.

TRUSON
Here. Try and write it down.

BOBBY JOBBY
Thank you Truson.

Bobby sets to writing on the piece of paper.

UNCLE TOMMY
(half-cut)
He's a dullard, can't write.

BOBBY JOBBY
I can write fine.

Bobby finishes, then presents the paper to Truson, who reads it out.

TRUSON
Sfinks sfinks sfinks sfinks sfinks.

UNCLE TOMMY
He's a muppet Truson. Leave it.

BOBBY
That's not what I wrote!

Bobby retrievesw the paper. He believed he was writing a description of The Object eating books, he is distraught by the evidence of the paper which Truson now holds up. It reads "Sfinx sfinx sfinx...", written in a childish hand.

UNCLE TOMMY
(slurring to himself)
Clearly this one's a tard.
(To Bobby, extending his glass for emphasis)
I can learn you to read and write Bobby. No? No need to thank me. Hic.

Truson puts the felt-tips in front of Bobby.

TRUSON
Sometimes I find it's easier to draw difficult things. Would you like to try and draw it, Bobby?

Bobby takes the felt tips and a new sheet of paper, and begins to scribble.

UNCLE TOMMY
(pointing, shakily)
It's because he's been having lessons from the Babydoll. The leggy blonde bitch. She herself can neither read nor write. She only learnt English ... 3 years ago. And she's frigid.

TRUSON
Uncle Tommy!

UNCLE TOMMY
(Hicupping)
Bob. I will gladlyhelp you to
(half singing, looking across at Babydoll)
read—and wife.

BOBBY JOBBY
I can read and write just fine thank you! I don't need any special treatment. I just don't trust books.

DADDY (V.O.)
And right you are Jobbins!

Daddy is at the bar, chips in.

DADDY (CONT.)
Right you are to view books with suspicion. Books are experiences prostituted! We simply do not know what we are looking at these days. Oh yeah, I would take the verbal over the visual any day. That's Plato, mate—and why I am writing my new play

IN MY MIND!!!
(to himself, as if measuring something significant)
Hmmm. Plato-Potato. Plato-Potato.

TOMMY
Fuck off Charlie.

Bobby holds his drawing up to Truson and Tommy.

BOBBY JOBBY
(optimistically)
There!

They pause, confused by the drawing.

TRUSON
But Bobby, that's just shapes and colours.

UNCLE TOMMY
Indeed. A chimp's turd could draw it better. Bobby, you need lessons.

TRUSON
Maybe it's a representation of an idea?

Bobby, frustrated and distressed, grabs the felt-tips and paper and staggers over to the workers table. He begins gesticulating and talking to them.

TRUSON
What's he doing Uncle Tommy?

TOMMY
He's reaching out to his fellow man.

Uncle Tommy burps.

From Uncle Tommy and Truson's P.O.V.: The workers are smiling bemusedly at Bobby. As he finishes talking one of them holds up a photograph of a Murano clown's face.

CUT TO:
CLOSE UP OF THE MURANO CLOWN HEAD PHOTOGRAPH.

WORKER *1
Did it look like this?

INT.—THE LIBRARY

The Object is noisily finishing more books—'Uses of Literacy' by Richard Hoggart and 'Agricultural Field Experiments' by Roger C. Petersen.

INT.—THE PUB

Daddy is speaking on Babydoll's mobile phone.

DADDY
Hello, Brian. I've done it. Today's
play. Yes. It's BECKETT-CANNON-BALL.
(Pause)
What's that? Hang on I can't hear you.
I'm down the pub.

DADDY
No Brian the director, you listen.
"Beckett-Cannon-Ball." No it's NOT the
title. That's the fucking play Pal.

It's 3 words. Minimal. Reduced. Think
music-hall, think existential! Think!?
Brian—don't be a tosser—start
workshopping this play at once or I
cut your funding and you go home to
bed, crying. How does that sound?
Right. That's better. Beckett. Cannon.
Ball. The wind of inspiration strikes!
Respondez, genius.

Daddy drops the mobile phone into half a pint of lager.

INT.—THE LIBRARY
INT.—INSIDE THE ROOF

Bobby Jobby is pasting some grout into a hole in the eaves in the roof. He is standing in an expansive, dark attic space—part of a large roof structure. Behind him a small, lumpen form begins to glow in the dark. An erratic reverberating dripping & plopping sound begins. Bobby hears the sound and turns around. He sees the distant glow and begins to move slowly, into the darkness. He reaches out with his arms to feel his way through the dark space, like a blind-man. After manouevring his way around a few obstructions he reaches the form.

BOBBY JOBBY
(to himself)
What would you say that is then?

It is a basic, foul-smelling lumpen, translucent shape with a dim, pulsing interior glow. It resembles a small pile of dung, but with a number of strange shaped protruberances. Bobby stares in awe at the form.

BOBBY JOBBY
That's very interesting.

He crouches down for a closer look. He reaches out and touches the surface, near the top—there is a pulpy discharge on top which is hardening in layers further down the mound. Bobby picks up some of the white substance on the end of his fingertips and smells it—it is acrid and unpleasant.

BOBBY JOBBY
Acrid. That could be ammonia.

CUT TO:

The Object, in the rafters. The Object is regurgitating small amounts of the white, gloopy substance—partially digested pages of the books it has eaten—into its cupped hand then reaching out and dispensing the liquid in squirts down into the darkness below.

CUT TO:

The liquid splats onto the top of a 2nd form, similar to the one Bobby is inspecting in an adjacent area of the attic. From a low position just behind this 2nd form we can see Bobby studying the other pile of matter—and that there are several other similarly shaped forms in-between the foregrounded 2nd form and the one Bobby is inspecting in the background. Periodically a splat of gunk lands on top of the form in the foreground.

CUT TO:

Bobby registers a sound and turns his head, thereby seeing the other glowing mounds in the adjacent area of the attic.

BOBBY JOBBY
What's that?

Navigating the dark space very carefully he walks across towards the mound which is being dripped onto from above. As he approaches it the dripping stops. He reaches it and looks up into the darkness, but can see nothing. He crouches to inspect the lump. Again it has a number of protruberances. Bobby reaches out, touches it, smells it and is repelled again.

BOBBY JOBBY

That's acrid. I'll say that could be ammonia.

CUT TO:

The Object regurgitating into its hand and dispensing the white, half-digested book-mulch into the space below from a different angle and position.

CUT TO:

we now see Bobby inspecting the 2nd form from behind a nearby 3rd form. It is now the 3rd form that is being dripped on from above. Bobby is enraptured by the 2nd form, and is studying it again, just as he did with the 1st form. The dripping-plopping sound continues. Bobby notices it.

BOBBY JOBBY

What's that sound there?

And carefully navigates the space again until he reaches the 3rd form, by which point the sound has again stopped. Bobby Jobby is again enraptured by the form...

BOBBY JOBBY

I'll say that's a familiar smell.

CUT TO:

... The Object has repositioned itself again. It regurgitates again into its hand. The cycle continues.

INT.—INSIDE THE ROOF
MONTAGE

FILM IN DARK SPACE IMAGES OF THE PICTOGRAPHIC SCULPTURES ACCUMULATING AND GROWING IN A DARK SPACE.

The Object spitting pulp into cupped hand.

The Object dispensing pulp by hand and by mouth, in different positions.

END OF EPISODE 2

EPISODE 3—"THE CURE OF FOLLY"

INT.—THE LIBRARY
INT.—THEATRE BACKSTAGE
INT.—THE GREENHOUSE
INT.—THE THEATRE
INT.—THE LIVING ROOM

Truson is standing in the living room in front of The Object, holding his Venus. The Object has a plant growing out of the top of its head and a muffied, guttural rumbling sound is emanating from its stomach. As Truson steps forward The Object begins making a rattling throaty noise, as if it were coughing but without opening its mouth. Truson puts the Venus replica on the floor and looks up at The Object.

TRUSON
If you talk to plants they can grow
better. Are you a plant?

The Object coughs up a pebble. It lands on the floor and rolls up to the Venus replica.

The Object's stomach is still making the rumbling sound. It gets louder as Truson steps over the Venus and pebble and walks slowly towards The Object.

TRUSON
Can I help you?

Truson reaches out to towards The Object, holding it at the sides and leaning in towards it. The muffied rumbling sound gets louder. Truson places his ear on The Object's stomach. He closes his eyes and listens to the sound. In his mind he begins to see three-dimensional text.

NOTE:
Use interpolating technique to display this text as regular 3-D subtitles on a pastoral country landscape background, with the guttural grumbling noise clearer and louder. We are seeing inside the body of The Object. Its stream of consciousness is articulated in the form of 3-D subtitles which Truson sees in his mind's eye.

Truson pulls his head away and blinks a few times. He repositions his head on The Object's stomach.

THE OBJECT (3-D SUBTITLE)
SFX: Delete-click-delete. Locale
Latinate. Classical cipher thickens
walls click, click, SHIFT. Qu'est-ce
que vous-voulez à manger? Something
under NOTHING. Negative zero, a hyphen
and a hole. You may have arrived too
late. L L L L L L L.
My editorial ambition is not local.
It has a generic application.

Truson, eyes close and face still resting on The Object's belly, pulls a surprised face. The Object coughs and spits paper-mulch onto his back.

TRUSON
What are you called?

THE OBJECT (3-D SUBTITLE)
I would define myself in relation to
them: I am not them. *(in morse code)*
All the Mick Clays are white, flat,
non-reflective forms. This series does
not stop at three dimensions, they
proceed into the 4th & 5th. *(singing)*
Daisy wheel, daisy wheel, I did love

thee. And now you are all encrusted
and be-jammed and broken. Daisy wheels
turn backwards. PAUSE FOR ONE DAY. The
herbaceous removal of thought is a
good line. PAUSE FOR ONE MONTH.
Realised today, the clock ticking in
the background is my own bloody sound
—own pulse. Damned environments.
PAUSE FOR ONE YEAR.

Truson, eyes closed and face resting on Object's stomach, looks very interested. The Object spits more paper-mulch onto his back.

INT.—DADDY'S STUDY
EXT.—THE WOODS
INT.—THE LIVING ROOM

END OF EPISODE 3

EPISODE 4—"INTERNAL PROBLEMS"

EXT.—BOBBY'S VAN

Bobby whistles and jingles his car keys as he strolls around the outside of the building. He turns to find his van has been further graffiti-ed with excrement and the words "Bobby Jobby CANT RIGHT" cover the top half of one side of the van. Bobby is shocked and stops in his tracks, jaw-dropping.

BOBBY JOBBY
(under his breath)
Oh the little bastard!
(shouting)
Miss Anna!!

BABYDOLL (V.O.)
Yes Bobby?

Babydoll is standing nearby, behind Bobby.

BABYDOLL (CONT.)
No need to shout.

Bobby points to the van, enraged.

BOBBY JOBBY
Gah!

Babydoll quickly begins laughing but brings her hand to her mouth to suppress it.

BOBBY JOBBY (CONT.)
It's not funny. You think you are but you're not.

BABYDOLL
(sweetly)
I'm sorry Bobby...

BOBBY JOBBY
"Bobby—Jobby—cannot—riggot. Cant write?! I can write.
(aggressively)
I can read and I can write alright Miss Anna!

Bobby turns away from her enraged, and looks at the ground.

BOBBY JOBBY
(to himself)
Driving home for Christmas.

BABYDOLL
Bobby! I didn't do this. Honestly Bobby, I hadn't seen the—harm done to your car—until that moment. But... can't you see the funny side?

BOBBY JOBBY
I don't believe it's not you!

BABYDOLL
It wasn't. I would tell you if it were me. I'm not frightened Bobby—but I am sorry about it though. Who could have done this that is not me? Maybe it was the neighbours, or a tinker, passing through the grounds?

BOBBY JOBBY
Tinkers!? You think it was knackers!? You think the Pavees would come in here and piss up my van with shit!? Do you know where I'm from?

BABYDOLL
(lighting a cigarette)
Leeds?

BOBBY JOBBY
You see! This is part of one of the games, isn't it? Christ-alive!

BABYDOLL
Come on Bobby. I'll help you clean it up. Maybe it was Daddy—it could be Daddy's idea of a funny. It doesn't matter much now though does it? Spilt milk. How much do you tink it will cost to clean it off?

BOBBY JOBBY
I think it'll cost about 200 pound I expect, for the valet.

BABYDOLL
I can help you with that Bobby. Can you take a cheque?

Babydoll produces a cheque from 1898. Bobby takes it and looks pleased with it, then leaves.

EXT.—BY BOBBY'S VAN

Truson is returning from picking up letter *3 at the garden perimeter.

He is approaching Babydoll.

TRUSON
Hello Babydoll! Bye Bobby!

Truson produces the letter from his pocket.

BABYDOLL
Hello Truson. What's that?

TRUSON
There were some people from the council here, outside the gate, and they left this letter for Daddy.

BABYDOLL
Another one. Can I see it?

TRUSON
Yes—it's in four parts—different colours look. It looks nice, but it's difficult to read.

Truson passes her the new letter from the council, this time it is issued in quadruplicate. There are various typed symbols and signs, a cluster of typed information, which looks like machine code. It is not readable in any conventional manner. Babydoll studies it.

BABYDOLL
He won't like this.

TRUSON
He's already very stressed.

Babydoll seems pleased.

BABYDOLL
He is isn't he? Truson—it might be better if I give it to him…when he's less upset.

Truson gives her the letter with some relief.

BABYDOLL (CONT.)
Truson wait—what do you think it is?

TRUSON
It's definitely information we don't understand. That's what's upsetting Daddy.

INT.—THE KITCHEN

Daddy is positioned very close to one of The Object's droppings in the kitchen. His tongue is poking out very slightly and touching the dropping. He is moving his head up and down on it. Babydoll enters the room, followed by Truson. Daddy recoils, defensively.

BABYDOLL
Charles! What on earth is that smell? What are you doing with those things?

Daddy seems quite wired. He stares at Babydoll, pie-eyed.

DADDY
Studying—I'm—learning from them!

She reaches into her pocket for the letter, but changes her mind.

BABYDOLL
Charlie darling they absolutely stink. We can't have them in the house.

DADDY
I am certain that these formations are a kind of text.

He moves very close to the dropping again, greedily.

DADDY (CONT.)
Must—translate.

BABYDOLL
Charles—we are not having those stinking things in the kitchen. They look like guano and smell like dog shit. You don't know what you're doing.

DADDY
Don't imply that! These are—these are psionic-amplifiers! I am inches away from an alchemical victory against the council, and these things—from the house—are here to help me!

Sniffing one.

DADDY (CONT.)
And they smell gooood!

BOBBY JOBBY
It might be better if we put them in the garden. Acrid, aren't they—like a bum. Fertilizer. They could be good for the roses. Sure I could burn them first to make sure.

DADDY
Burn them? Burn them?? Do you want to burn the Rosetta Stone too, moron?! Or how about the Dead Sea Scrolls.
Oh, take the night off, Jobson!
Pssshh! Out prole, out!

EXT.—BOBBY'S VAN

Bobby is rattling his car keys as he marches, chuntering angrily to himself, around the outside of the building.

BOBBY JOBBY
Definitely gonna pick up some drinks for the wife.

He turns to find his van has been further graffiti-ed and the words "Bobby Jobby CANT RIGHT and there is a penis sign" cover the entirety of the driver's side of the van—which is facing Bobby. He is shocked and stops in his tracks.

BOBBY JOBBY
Who? Wha? Oh no...

Bobby crouches despondently. Looking up at the van his mood changes to anger. He becomes resolute and picks himself up.

BOBBY JOBBY
Definitely going to go and pick up some drinks for the wife.

Feeling self-conscious about the graffiti, Bobby approaches the van, gets into the driver's side and starts the engine. He does not see the passenger side of the van. He reverses and pulls away. We see there is a large cartoon penis smeared onto the passenger side of the van, in an adolescent style.

INT.—PUB TOILETS / OFFICE

Daddy—very drunk, enters the pub toilets.

DADDY
I'll just get the old tailey out.

Daddy unzips his flies.

DADDY (CONT.)
(addressing his penis)
And I'm going to do a wee-wee out of it.

He sees other men at the urinals.

DADDY (CONT.)
Well we'd better get a cubicle,
hadn't we Tailey?

Daddy opts for a cubicle.

There is dry ice coming out from under the cubicle, and a glowing light. Daddy reaches out to the cubicle door.

DADDY (CONT.)
I don't know how other men cope.
He opens the cubicle door and is swathed in fog.

MICK JAGGER (V.O.)
Alright Charlie.

DADDY
Who's that? Mick?

All the Micks speak in unison:

MICK JAGGER
Yes

MICK FLEETWOOD
Yes

MICK HUCKNALL
Yes

MICK JAGGER
Come inside me old Chum-Mucker

Daddy enters the cubicle. The mists clear and Daddy finds himself in a kind of enhanced office environment. It could be an office for a very cool design company. There are 3 desks. Each desk has a secretary working at it. The secretaries are overweight middle-aged men. Standing in the fore-ground are, from left to right, Mick Hucknall, Mick Jagger and Mick Fleetwood.

MICK JAGGER (CONT.)
This is small Mick and this is tall Mick. And those are our home secretaries.

DADDY
(slurring)
Micks? How did you get inside my house?

MICK JAGGER
What are you on Charlie? You're inside our house.

MICK FLEETWOOD
We thought you might be having problems with your nought.

DADDY
My nought? I haven't got a nought.

MICK HUCKNALL
See! I told you he'd deny it!
(more quietly, to the other two Micks)
We shouldn't be talking to him about the nought without the proper paperwork.

DADDY
(ovehearing, confused)
Paperwork?

MICK JAGGER
Oh no...

DADDY
That's square!

MICK HUCKNALL
Square? Square!? I'll tell you what's square—

Mick Hucknall runs at Daddy and attacks his leg, slapping and scratching it

MICK HUCKNALL (CONT.)
marginalising yourself and being absolutely effing useless while I win!

Mick Hucknall tries to bite him

MICK HUCKNALL (CONT.)
Rarrghh-ghghnnghh-rarggh.

DADDY
Aaargghhhh! Get off my leg!

MICK FLEETWOOD
(smiling into space)
Naughty!

MICK JAGGER
(to Mick Fleetwood)
Mick!

Mick Jagger snaps his fingers—Mick Fleetwood responds as if programmed.

MICK FLEETWOOD
Control. This. Woman.

Mick Fleetwood picks Mick Hucknall up by the hair and then kicks him in the arse, sending him spinning off into the wall.

MICK HUCKNALL
(brushing himself down)
Sorry, Micks. Sorry. It's just that
that kind of talk really infuriates me.

MICK JAGGER
*(clapping his hands together,
as if to assert order)*
Charlie—we've got a proposition for
you, haven't we guys—

MICK HUCKNALL
Oh yes!

MICK FLEETWOOD
Very difficult choices for women.

Mick Hucknall looks irritated with Mick Fleetwood.

Daddy approaches Mick Jagger cautiously eyeing Mick Fleetwood.

DADDY
(whispering and pointing)
I don't understand what that one is saying.

MICK HUCKNALL
Don't start ganging up and being anti social.

MICK JAGGER
We're forming—A NEW BAND!

MICK FLEETWOOD
In a breakthrough year for women.

MICK HUCKNALL
(to Mick Fleetwood)
Do it properly! There's no point if you're not going to do it properly!

DADDY
(confused)
A new brand?

MICK HUCKNALL
No a new band a new band a new band!

DADDY
A...supergroup?

MICK JAGGER
That's exactly right. We'll sing—and we wanted to invite you—to play—

MICK FLEETWOOD
(as if it were a magic word)
Marimba!

Mick Hucknall produces various papers

MICK HUCKNALL
And you'll also have the title of "Honorary Titular Concilliary of Ourhouse"—because we are all going to have these unusual names—just sign here, here, here, here and ....here!

DADDY
Far out! What's the band called?

MICK FLEETWOOD
It's called "S.S. Sanhedrin"

DADDY
Sanhedrin? Sanhedrin? Is that the council is it? I'm not working for the council, I can't let them into Ourhouse Mick, they'll fuck it all up.

MICK HUCKNALL
(enraged again)
Oh this really gets my goat!

MICK JAGGER
Chill Charlie chilly-chill-chill.

MICK HUCKNALL
Narrow minded!

MICK FLEETWOOD
Very, very difficult choices for women.

MICK JAGGER
Look Chuck. You've got a problem with your buhject, right?

DADDY
What? Buh—my books?

MICK FLEETWOOD
No your nought

MICK JAGGER
Exactly! And we can help you with that. We know where the problem lies...

DADDY
What? Where are they?
MICK FLEETWOOD
Look to the earth!

MICK HUCKNALL
Earth! Earth! Earth!

MICK JAGGER
Your problem is OUTSIDE. And the thing about this council is—it's INSIDE. And it's run by a really great bunch of guys.

DADDY
What? You?

MICK JAGGER
That's all it is Chucky-Muck.

Daddy looks impressed.

DADDY (CONT.)
Girls! Come over here and help Charlie relax.

The middle-aged male 'secretaries' approach Daddy and gaze into his eyes. Two of them take him by a hand each.

DADDY
Uh....uh! Wow!

The 3rd secretary raises his hand and puts it on top of Daddy's head.

MICK JAGGER
The Sanhedrin is just a groovy place—where all your dreams come true.

DADDY
Far-out!

MICK HUCKNALL
It's your birth-right Charles. Why not enjoy it?

HOME SECRETARY*3
Don't worry Daddy—you are hallucinating.

The 3 Micks and the Secretaries laugh. Daddy is in an ecstatic state.

MICK FLEETWOOD
Can I smash him now?

MICK JAGGER
No need Mick, no need.

INT.—DADDY'S BEDROOM

Daddy walks into the bedroom, apparently quite high. He is impersonating Mick Jagger.

DADDY
Hello love.

He tries to kiss her, she swats him away.

DADDY
We've got a problem with our B-Ject.
Give us a kiss.

BABYDOLL
What's a buhject? You're drunk.
You stink.

Babydoll holds her hand up to him.

BABYDOLL
Don't.

DADDY
Come on wifey, I've just been
seriously turned on.

BABYDOLL
No!

Babydoll begins to beat him.

BABYDOLL
Don't you get wiggley! Don't you get wiggley again! Don't make me do this to you Daddy!

She punches him to the floor.

DADDY
Fantastic. I love you.

He passes out.

EXT.—GREENHOUSE, NIGHT

Bobby Jobby returns to Ourhouse in his van. He is drunk. He falls out of his van, slipping on empty lager cans.

BOBBY JOBBY
I'm feeling vexed now!
I'm back at your service you pair of bastards!
Is your hearing broken!?
(noticing a goat in the field behind a nearby fence)
How's it going Vincent?

Bobby staggers into his greenhouse carrying some empty bin liners and the lagers. He retrieves about 30 books that he has hidden inside the greenhouse. The books Bobby has chosen to bury are a fairly kitsch selection. He dumps these into bin liners in his wheelbarrow along with a couple of sacks of earth. He then puts his Sony walkman on, creating a soundtrack of intense acid-house music, insulating himself with sound.

BOBBY
Now I'm back!

He takes on, a focused look as he wheels his wheelbarrow out into the garden. He begins digging.

END OF EPISODE FOUR

EPISODE 5—"COUNCIL SERVICES"

INT.—THE LIVING ROOM

Daddy runs into the lounge wearing colourful baggy body builders' 'pants' and tank top. He runs in circles around The Object. The Object has changed position again. It is half-way between kneeling and standing. With one hand it is holding a spade at the angle and position of an erection, as if it were about to hit something. Its other hand dangles, loose. The earth which was partially covering The Object when Bobby saw it on its knees the day before, has been swept into the four corners of the room. The Object is smiling. Daddy drops to the floor and starts doing press ups. His arms are looking very pumped.

DADDY
(to himself)
Help!

Daddy continues to do press ups. He is grunting and sweating.

DADDY (CONT.)
Listen mate, I've been wanting to talk
with you. I'm having a few—issues.

Daddy gets up and starts running on the spot.

DADDY (CONT.)
Small, administrative problems really—
not a big deal—but the thing is the
timing. The timing is just not all
that great and I'm feeling—

Daddy jogs up close to The Object and continues running on the spot, but reaches out and pokes The Object's face and chest as he does so.

DADDY (CONT.)
God you're looking buff! No, seriously
you look great!

Daddy jogs backwards and begins doing standing jumps, facing The Object from a position a couple of metres away from it.

DADDY
Anyway, so I was feeling sort of under
pressure. A bit stressed out. BUT!
I think I know where my books have
been going.

Daddy stops jumping.

DADDY (CONT.)
And I'm going to get the fucker. Oh
yes I am! Will-you-help-me?

Daddy start jogging again. He jogs up to The Object and stops in front of it very close.

DADDY
The offender must be punished! You are
cool. You are cool!

Daddy attempt to high-five The Object's dangling hand. It is not raised—it just flops and hangs, swinging a bit. Daddy tries again with little success, but his enthusiasm is undiminished.

DADDY
Woo! Yeah! Alright!

Daddy jogs out of the room.

INT.—THE LIVING ROOM, NIGHT (UN-PLACED SCENE)

In his night-wear—pyjamas and dressing gown, Daddy is talking to The Object whilst attempting to smoke a pipe. Daddy begins to speak with a northern accent.

DADDY
Brenda, I have been experiencing
certain social—feelings—that I
would like to share with you. My
family would not understand—because
I have cushioned them against—
aspects of life.

He produces a small notebook and pencil from his dressing gown pocket.

DADDY (CONT.)
Charlie Maddox-Wilson, "On suffering
by approximation".
(lighting his pipe)
Where is the rich man who will say
"it's been easy for me?"
(puffing smoke)
Isn't it possible that in every little
life, everyone feels a similar sense
of strife? Is there an 'axiom of
suffering' that all men will achieve
to justify their sentiment; whether
they've been born to privilege and
manage it through exaggeration of mild
injury, vapours, depressions etc.- or,
being born to misery, level it through
stoic and pugilistic understatement?
In short—doesn't everyone, no matter
what their lot, through mental and
gymnastic assimilation, feel they
suffer in roughly equal clumps?

If 'yes', then ipso facto—no-one has
a worse time than anyone else.

EXT.—THE GARDEN

Bobby is in the garden, shovelling earth into a wheelbarrow. He falls over in pain and picks himself back up, clutching his leg and continues.

Limping and hopping he wheels the barrow full of earth into the house.

He emerges from the house with an empty barrow. He picks up his spade and hurts his arm, grabs it in pain, and slips and hurts his leg again. He picks himself up and begins shovelling the earth from the ground into the barrow again, despite being in considerable physical pain.

Bobby, hobbling and hopping, wheels another full barrow of earth into the house.

Bobby wheels another empty barrow of earth from the house into the garden.

Bobby collapses again, falling into the wheelbarrow.

INT.—THE KITCHEN

Daddy is close to Babydoll, speaking in a conspiratorial manner.

DADDY
Do you think it could be Robert Jobson
who's been taking them?

BABYDOLL
Bobby?- he can't read! Why would he...

DADDY

Some other reason perhaps...maybe he secretly hates me. I am his employer after all. Tommy suggested I keep an eye on him, and then last night, after the pub I saw Mick Jagger and he hinted that I had a problem that was something to do with the earth! Bobby is the gardener, and he's been digging everything up!

BABYDOLL

That's true—and today he's been bringing earth into the house.

DADDY

Why's he doing that?

BABYDOLL

"Repairs".

DADDY

Christ!

BABYDOLL

And, Daddy, and...I didn't know how to tell you, but I saw him with a book.

DADDY

What?!

BABYDOLL

He was reading a book called "Learning To Read". Which I thought was a bit—

DADDY
Suspicious

BABYDOLL
Very suspicious. You should look through his things, see if you can find any evidence. Who would have thought it—loyal Bobby, turning against you.

DADDY
We don't know that yet, for sure, do we darling...

BABYDOLL
Well...

DADDY
(suddenly very angry)
If this is true then Robert Jobson is an absolute shit! And we must plan for his come-uppence.

EXT.—THE GARDEN

Truson is sitting on a fallen tree trunk, surrounded by mud and various dead birds. He is holding his Venus facsimile and crying. The Venus is muddied. Truson's faith in his father has been shaken by his father's behaviour the night before, and the effect of his own photography on the birds. Babydoll approaches him.

TRUSON
(sniffing)
They all died.

Truson is holding a bird and its polaroid.

TRUSON (CONT.)
Does lightning kill birds?

Babydoll strokes his hair.

BABYDOLL
Sometimes I think. But not often.

TRUSON
My photographs killed them all.

He drops his sculpture into the mud.

BABYDOLL
No they didn't....shhhh.

Hugging him.

TRUSON
With Daddy's camera.

BABYDOLL
Maybe. Maybe. That's terrible. Here—
your sculpture of the lady.

She picks up the muddied Object.

TRUSON
I don't want it.

BABYDOLL
Come on Truson—it's beautiful.

TRUSON
Faxon and Daddy said it's not real,
they said it's fake.

He starts crying.

TRUSON
Are you going to leave Daddy?

BABYDOLL
(surprised)
I...I....

She gathers herself.

BABYDOLL
Truson. I need you to be strong now. You can be strong, can't you? Listen to me. You are very special.

He smiles, bleary eyed.

TRUSON
Am I?

BABYDOLL
And this is real fake. Do you understand?

TRUSON
No.

BABYDOLL
It's a powerful, powerful thing.

TRUSON
Really?

BABYDOLL
Really. You can do a lot with it.

Truson produces Babydoll's 'major project' book, that he found.

TRUSON
I've got your book. I made a drawing of you in it. You won't leave, will you?

Babydoll touches him on the cheek and kisses his forehead.

BABYDOLL
No.

INT.—GREENHOUSE

Babydoll is sitting with Bobby in the greenhouse again.

BOBBY JOBBY
I've got an idea for a film

BABYDOLL
Really Bobby, what's it about?

BOBBY JOBBY
It's about these guys that pick up this hitch-hiking monkey. It's like a road-movie.

BABYDOLL
Like the Clint Eastwood film

BOBBY JOBBY
Yeah but with a real monkey.

BABYDOLL
Everywhich Way But Loose

BOBBY JOBBY
And anyway, they pick-up this monkey—it's a real monkey—and it can talk.

BABYDOLL
But the monkey in Everywhich Way But Loose was a real monkey.

BOBBY JOBBY
No that was just a guy in a suit, following Clint Eastwood.

BABYDOLL
No Bobby it was a real Orang-Utang. Clyde the Orang-Utang.

BOBBY JOBBY
It wasn't it was just a really good suit. Anyway they pick up this monkey—a real one—and it starts talking to them. It can talk, like.

BABYDOLL
But Bobby—monkeys can't talk.

BOBBY JOBBY
I know—it's great isn't it. It's a magic monkey. It starts talking with them, freaking them out. Fucking with their heads.

BABYDOLL
Where are you going to get a real talking monkey from Bobby?

BOBBY JOBBY
I dunno. What do you think?

BABYDOLL
Well—maybe someone could play the monkey.

BOBBY JOBBY
Like in the Clint Eastwood films? That's not a bad idea.

END OF EPISODE FIVE

Wall Eyed Stranger: An Introduction to Mellorfilm and the British Grotesque Explosion

BY
MICK PETER

Hep Talk and/or He Leaned His Head on My Shoulder and Inhaled the Spirited Stench of Meadow Lane (as if it were New Mexico).[1]

Heat percolated through to the surface of the face, its head leaning a little too hard into his shoulder. He thought about the nose, taught, shiny and pitted like a ripe strawberry, each open pore holding an impacted seed. His eyes rolled and wandered down avenues of hot straw. Absentmindedly he reached out for the cigarette. The strawberry became a sunburnt man, bellicose in a rancid vest.

PART ONE:

> I wondered why you always got less groupie attention than him. I mean he was about fifty… and wretched.

Brian[2] ranted like a madman, except he was quite a good ranter actually. He was supposed to be demented though, about not having found the type of suit he wanted to be wearing. 'Man, eurghhhhh' he kept saying, 'eurghhhh.' But he kept going, making odd little sounds to himself and smiling while Unipart[3] crouched beside him, nodding his head approvingly, and drumming his fingers on the flight case.[4] Sometimes he would belch too, not forcing it, just a couple of parps and a yawn. Brian was becoming Object.

'Hey man, this is bad', said Unipart. Appearing from behind a shack, Cooke didn't say anything at all, just hung back, kicking the dried dirt to bring up the dust. Unipart and Cooke were both wearing flesh-coloured body suits[5] as they always did, even at the pool.

'Hey man, no', he said, 'this is good man. This is theatre blood[6] you dig?

You'll find this helpful.' Unipart frowned. Cooke was still kicking the dirt. 'Blood', he said, getting behind the camera[7] again. They got started. Unipart squatted down to half face Cooke, he had begun to come round to the idea, or perhaps was beginning to dig the script.

'Sure man, that is true.' He smoothed his hair. 'Fake blood, crazy.' 'It's true', he told Cooke as he was disappearing behind a cloud. 'What is it man?' Cooke shouted, unseen, 'this First Blood?'

'Fake Blood! Fake Blood!' bellowed Unipart, cackling. 'That's far out man.'

The Script Writers' Concept Book by Simon Theame

At last they were in the bright interior. An upturned stool pointed its rubber hooves to the sky in the corner where Tape was leaning to watch the rainwater tumbling down the windows. He had a loose careless manner, yet a certain threat too, an almost imperceptible frown that said, 'things aren't going to work out.' Even though everyone had heard him speak before, they almost always laughed, because of the way he told it, the way he scowled as he intoned his latest writing, and the deranged way he delivered the proclamation 'I have a recurring nightmare that there is a snake in my toilet. A shit-eating snake. Feasting upon my becomingness!' making it almost incomprehensible.[8]

PART TWO:

'That ain't no ordinary radio transmission' said Tape,[9] 'that is Subject, that what that is.'

'What you doin'?, making some kind of art film?'

Subject appeared. Subject was a non-entity, a trope, a trick of a non-thing. Transforming himself from a can of warm lager (*see* **NOTE 6**) and taking the shape of a critic wearing delicately pointed shoes; he sashayed over to the corner of the studio and pulled out a wad of crumpled paper from under a corroded polystyrene monolith.[10]

'You reckon it's dried out enough?' Tape asked, sounding conciliatory as he squatted down beside Subject.

'Course not', said Subject, smiling helpfully in turn, and brushing the papers with his hands, 'you got to read it just when it's written, that's the purpose of the script, you see, that what we call *that.*'

He stood uncomfortably at the low table with biro in hand. He shielded the papers with his other arm. With furtive looks toward Tape he began to edit the text, cutting away the florid flab and archaic effulgence from the already overburdened, overwrought awfulness.[11]

'Sure do seem to be easy with that editorialising' said Tape; he walked round the table to get a better view. 'Look like some kinda neo-fascist modernism to me' he said laughing. 'Apes with eye patches an' sheet', he added for good measure.[12]

'Don't gen'lly take too much time', Subject commented casually, chewing the mangled pen lid, 'the critics say that if it's complicated it ain't worth sittin' through-they reckon it's got to be easy to be strong you see what I'm saying?'

They started outside for the bicycles, the papers now wrapped in a wad of carrier bags.

Tape spat.

In the distance, on the playing fields, a Viking in shaggy furs was being reprimanded.[13]

75% Off Your Next Lethal Injection When You Book in Advance with MSUMSCM*

*the management of a sustainable universe in the majestic and stunning classrooms of your mind.

Are you thinking of a career with a wider view, painful shouting and abject desolation and abandonment? For information on this and other ritualised practices please write to the University of Castle Hateball, H-Block, Civic Quarter, Leeds, LS1 3HE and request our leather-bound brochure sometime this century. We offer more in the way of sports, spurts and hurts than any other non-legal quasi-mediaeval establishment. One to one modularised master classes with a Turdule of your choice give you an opportunity to gain first hand experience of Prince Lightning's teachings.[14]

PART THREE: DANCING OUTSIDE MY TROUSERS

The experimental British music artist tells Weary Hack why musical territories do not discourage him. He's committed to not being washed away in the mainstream like so many enfeebled trout.

'We spend our lunchtimes being put into boxes, man. It's the boxes I hate.' It doesn't take much to get Dancing Outside My Trousers (aka Johnny

Vivash) talking in circles as we converse over a bag of wheat-grass sweets in his favourite London eatery *Intestinal Radiance.* This freckle-faced savant has consistently worried about boxes, moulds etc., combining impenetrable lyrics with non-hook laden ten-minute choruses from god knows where. 'This approach is wildly derivative' he opines. 'This collection was Steve Reich meets Norman Foster in leather and that just freaks people out. I don't shy away from the fact that I hate music. I'm not worried about just writing a pork pie commercial if I felt like it.'

Aside from his microcassette only releases, Dancing's previous albums *Literary Beard* and *College Ornament* sold horribly. The idea behind new album *The Unattractive One* has evolved from *La Philosophie dans le Boudoir.* No one made it a basis for their albums before and Dancing's vision is unlikely to help on tracks such as *The Descent* and *Significance.*

'I wanted to approach this like I was vomiting clay', he grimaces, 'To me *La Philosophie dans le Boudoir* was more like a telephone directory than fiction.' *The Unattractive One* is a horrendous listen by anyone's standards. Lead single *Ideas Need Emergency Surgery* has already become a storming concert-hall flop.

Dancing Outside My Trousers shares his grim outlook with fellow musician Ye Olde Crumhorn, who is similarly disengaged from doing anything good – and both have potentially made zero impact on their commercial acceptance as a result. He twitches involuntarily, 'whenever lunch is this bad I tend to leave. I'd probably be King Cnut [15] or Jay-Z or King Crimson [16] or King Kadmus [17] if I was more interesting.'

In *La Philosophie dans le Boudoir,* somebody says 'Fuck! Fuck! Come when you wish – for I can withstand it no longer! Oh double name of God be-fucked! Sacred bugger-God! I come! – Inundate me, my friends, soak drench, drown your whore! Spray floods of your scum-fuck to the very seat of this blazing soul! It exists for nought but to be slaked, quenched by your tides! Aië! Aië! Aië!' With *The Unattractive One*, Dancing Outside My Trousers is of his time-and, like, just beyond it too. [18]

Notes

1. Meadow Lane 'The Jimmy Sirrel Stand, Meadow Lane' (not the starting point for the 1969 'psych' concept album, Wonderlane, by Captain Techworm[1A]) is the home ground of Notts County, the self-styled 'oldest football club in the league.'

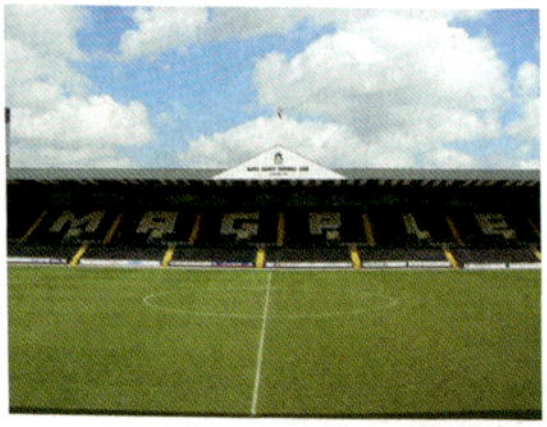

The Jimmy Sirrel Stand, Meadow Lane

Arsenal F.C. and Notts County F.C. logos

Mellors has a split loyalty between Notts County and Arsenal football clubs (a standpoint representative of the new Realpolitik). Mellors attended a football match in which a comedy banner [1B] was unveiled by his cousin, a certain Julian Morris (a sign-writer by trade and quoted as saying, 'I'm not a football fan, I'm a Notts County fan'). In a striking coincidence the banner concerned former Arsenal [1C] player Sol Campbell.

2. Brian, who will appear in *Ourhouse* (2010-), [2A] is a virile practitioner of high standing who has permitted himself to be degraded to further the Mellors canon.

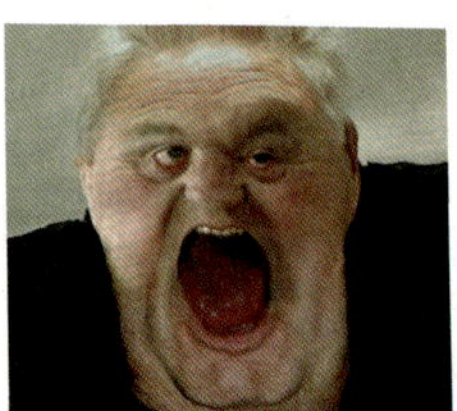

The Object (played by Brian Catling) facial distortion proposal by Tom Lauten

3. The Unipart legend has been explored to some degree but merits further fleeting commentary. We have established, in particular, that it was the derelict Oxford site [3A] of the car parts manufacturer.

Unipart logo

The source of much object repurposing [3B] was also the site of a quasi-mystical occurrence in the late nineteen nineties involving M, C, D and J. A fire was made on the concrete floor of a disused warehouse. As the stones exploded in the heat, J pushed C in ever decreasing circles in an engineless forklift truck as C sang extracts from famous operatic arias. D and M shielded their eyes from the flying debris.

4. Associated with the itinerant life of a touring musician. Often with band logo crudely stencilled onto it for identification and/or covered with stickers. [4A]

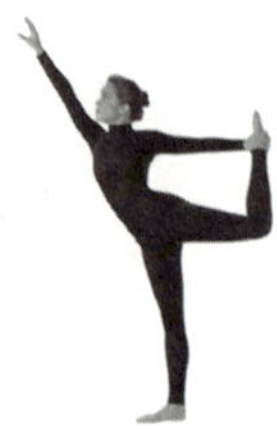

A body stocking or 'unitard'

5. Supplied by: Dancewear Solutions
6730 Manchester Avenue
St. Louis, MO 63139, USA [5A]

6. There are numerous instances of fake blood in Mellors' output. It first appears in *First Blood No.6* (2005) (part of *Hateball*).

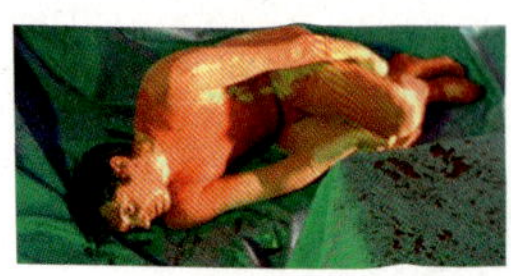

Johnny Vivash performs First Blood No.6.

In this work it was sprayed from a gardening pump in an arc across the studio, over the top of the camera and onto the performer by the artist whilst filming. In *Tokyo Rambo* (2006)

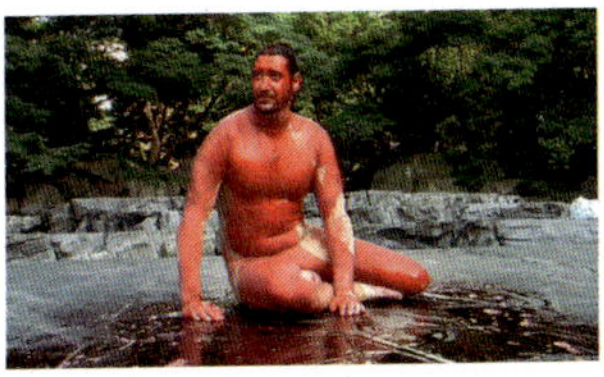

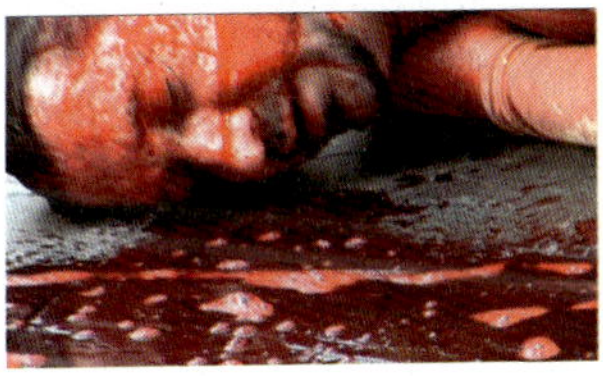

John Miller performs Tokyo Rambo

in order to achieve a more consistent flow further pumps were acquired from the Tokyu Hands megastore's gardening department. These were operated by the Grizedale Arts production crew.

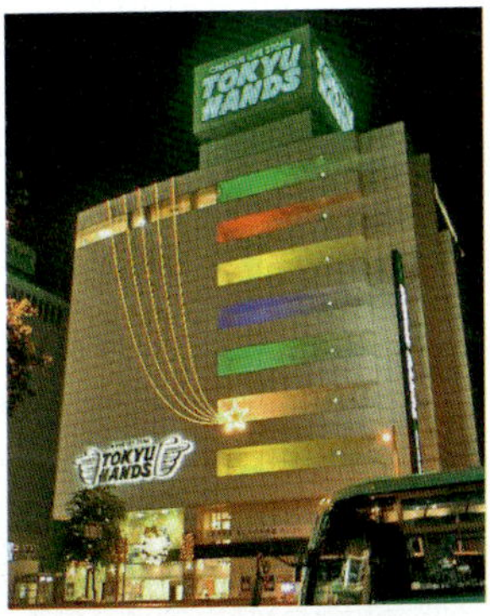

Tokyu Hands megastore

In *The Time Surgeon* (2007) fake blood, as well as a quantity of lager, was plumbed into a Sony TCM 939 tape recorder to spurt out of the headphone socket and out of the open cassette-loading tray. These spurts were controlled by medical valves attached to nylon tubes; medical and gardening equipment being used in wry combination.

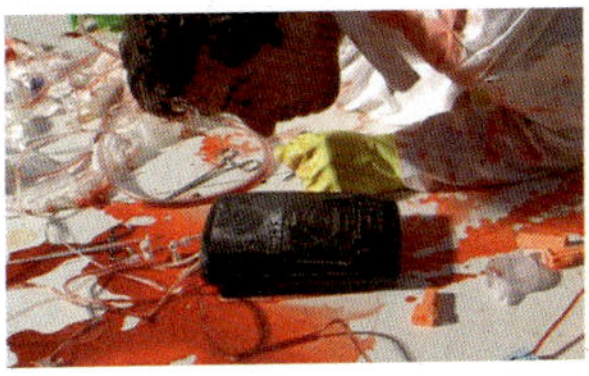

Blood and lager leak from the Sony TCM 939 in The Time Surgeon

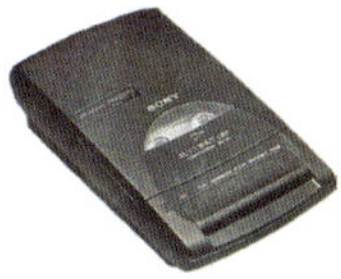

Sony TCM 939

7. List of cameras:

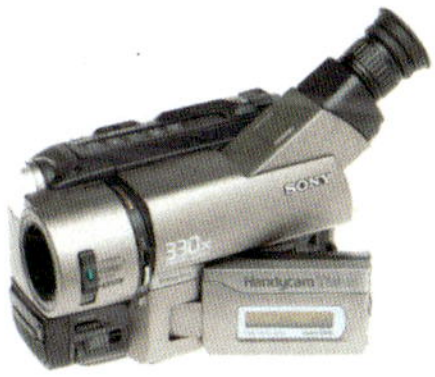

Sony Hi-8

I. Sony Hi-8 – Purchased by the artist in the summer of 1997, which he did use for all early video from his first installation

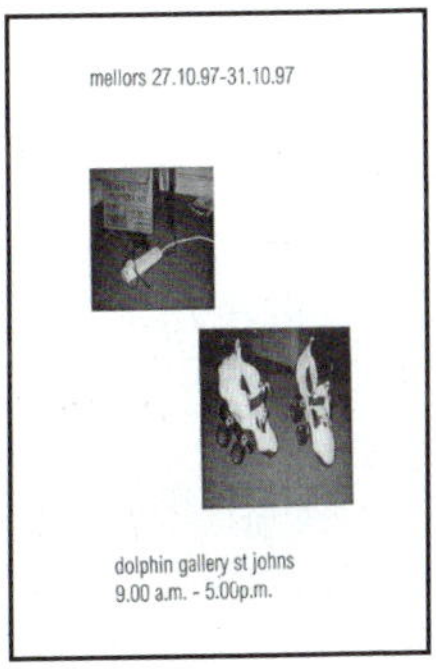

Exhibition poster

Mellors 27.10.97 – 31.10.97 Dolphin Gallery St. Johns to *Black Gold* at Matt's Gallery (2001), at which point it was being superseded by the emerging Mini DV format.

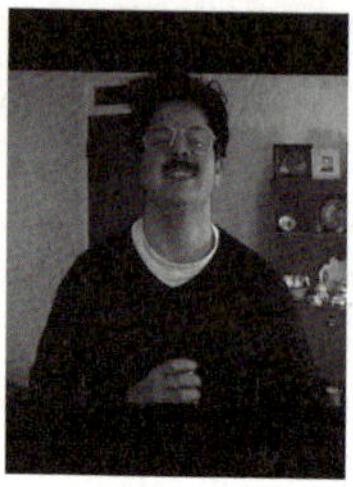

Black Gold, Matt's Gallery invitation card, 2001

Mellors has forgotten the specific Hi-8 model but recollects that it 'made all the colours brighter, which was good. Its cassette loader kept breaking though.'

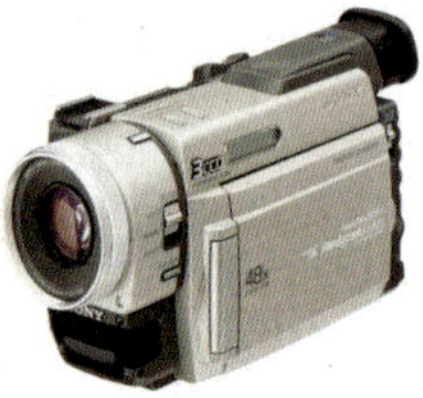

Sony TRV 900E

II. Sony TRV 900E – Purchased circa 1999 – first used to make the collaborative work *Basic Life Support* (1999) in which Mellors, wearing enormous leg extensions with wheels on the end and Size 17 basketball boots, was pushed around Tesco's (Canada Water) car-park like a trolley by Dan Fox, Ben Sadler, Andy Cooke and Tim Braden.

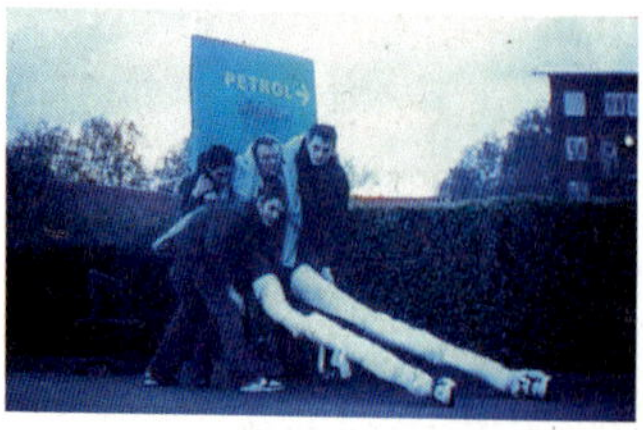

Still from Basic Life Support, 1999

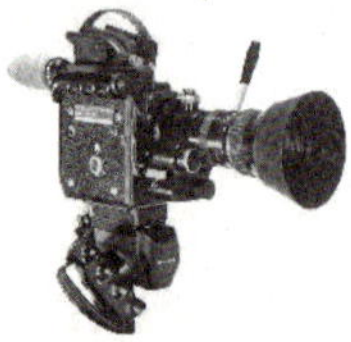

Bolex H-16 EBM Electric

III. Bolex H-16 EBM Electric system, belonging to Dan Fox. '(It) combines brilliant reflex viewing/focusing with 5-speed electronic drive and complete sync-sound capabilities; accepts accessory marine housing, 400' film magazine, and other Bolex system components.' Mellors first used this in 2002 for *Pod War* (The Landscape Critics) and then in 2004 for the video *Lab 75* (part of the installation *Profondo Viola*) which was filmed with Darren Flook & Holly Walsh performing Mellors' script inside Matt's Gallery, up the river by the canal outside Matt's Gallery, and in Victoria Park near Matt's Gallery (some relaxing footage of a fountain and a heron in a pond).[7A] Flook portrays the eponymous 'Man' who, armed only with a photocopy of a member of Dutch prog-rock group Focus

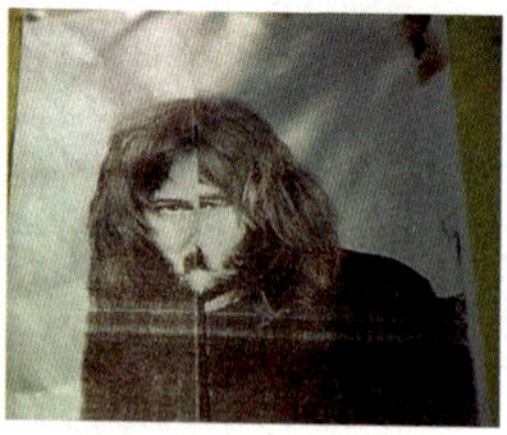

A photocopy of Jan Akkerman

and a large turnip, claims to be investigating progressive-rock as a cover for political evil.

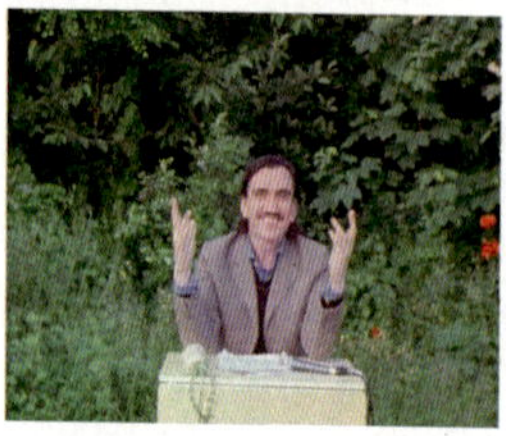

'Man'

Walsh portrays a miniature version of the Flook character ('Micro-Busey')

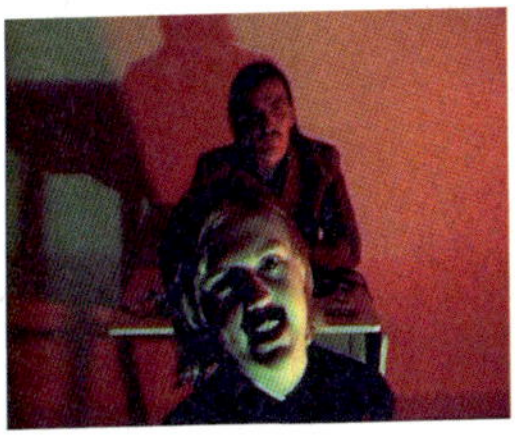

'Micro-Busey'

who later transubstantiates into a massive white plastic mountain and reads an emotive and self-conscious poem about Kevin Bacon ('POEM').[7B]

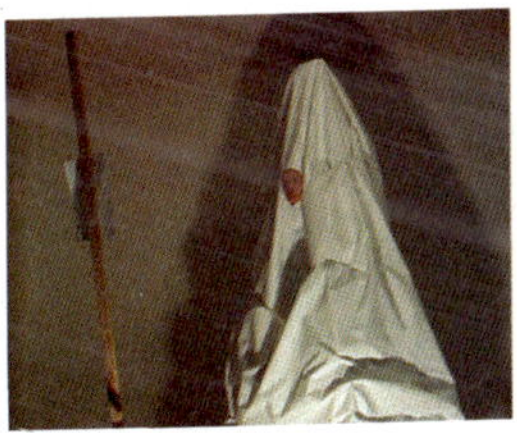

White plastic mountain reads POEM

Flook initially declared Mellors' script to be 'complete nonsense' but was sporting enough to participate and turned in a performance of some conviction.
Mellors also used the H-16 in 2005 for *Hateball* and in 2007 for *The Lowry Block*, which was cancelled by Berwick Gymnasium for its fictive portrayal of Lowry (played by Barney Mellors) as a racist who recounts a politically incorrect joke.[7C]

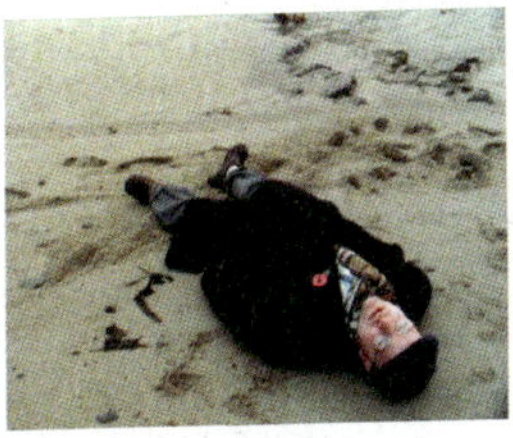

Barney Mellors as L.S. Lowry

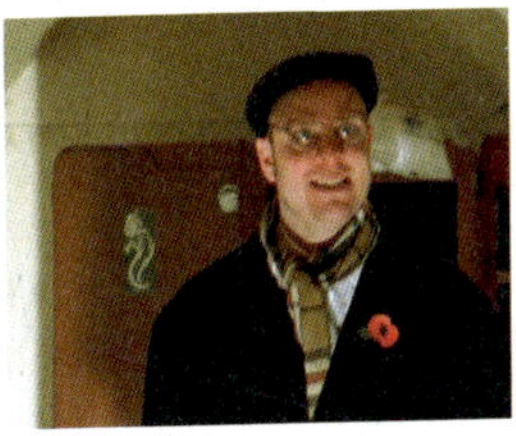

Barney Mellors as L.S. Lowry

Mellors' final use of the Fox Bolex H-16 was in 2007 for *The Time Surgeon*

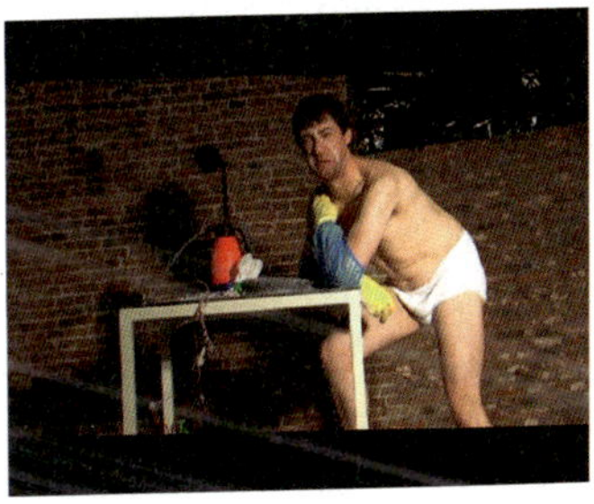

The Time Surgeon

– in which 16 mm footage is edited with Super-16, PAL DV and HDV formats, the resultant video jumps between 4:3, 16:9 and a unique aspect ratio just off 4:3 (the result of an accident in the telecine process).

IV. Since 2007 Mellors has worked in HD, which he considers 'more contemporary, less Modern'.

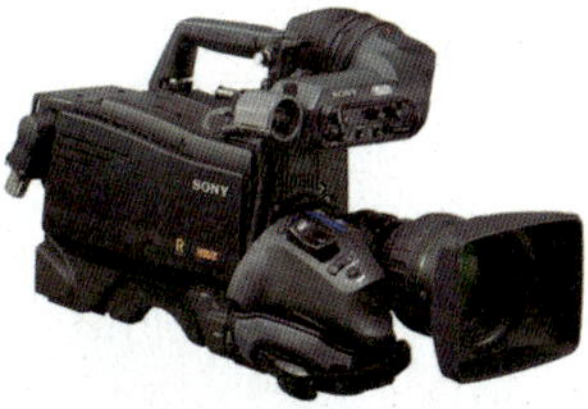

an HD camera

8. An impassioned plea in *The Ill-Tempered Manifesto* or *A New Aging Manifesto* or *The New Old Manifesto* delivered by Nathaniel Mellors at the Serpentine *Manifesto Marathon* on Saturday 18th October 2008.[8A]

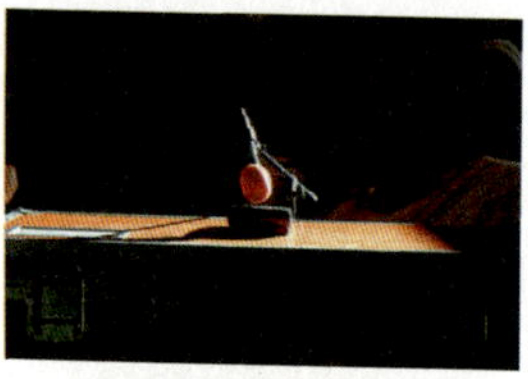

The Ill-Tempered Manifesto, Serpentine Gallery, 2008

9. Tape is an entity in *The Time Surgeon.*[9A]

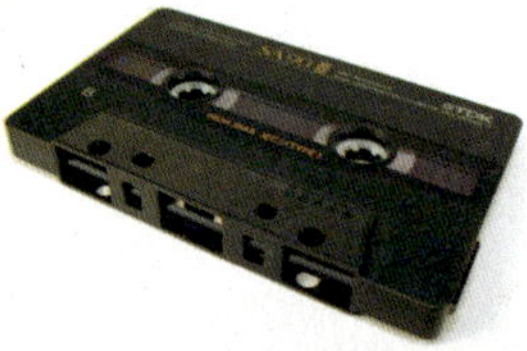

Tape

10. A large block of polystyrene in Mellors' Amsterdam studio, a material Mellors used to improvise large sculptural/architectural forms in *Profondo Viola* (2004). Videos were projected onto and over these forms.

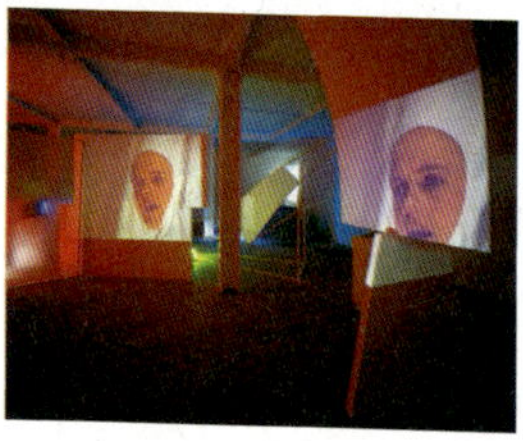

Polystyrene used to improvise sculpture and architectural forms in Profondo Viola

Mellors subsequently used an enormous polystyrene block for the projection of the abortive *The Lowry Block* (2007) and two thinner,

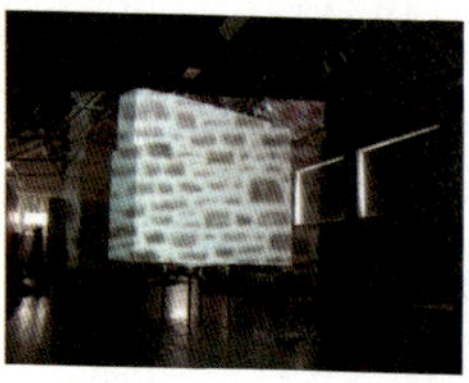

The Lowry Block projection test, Berwick Gymnasium

parallel blocks for the projection of one channel of *The Time Surgeon* (2007).

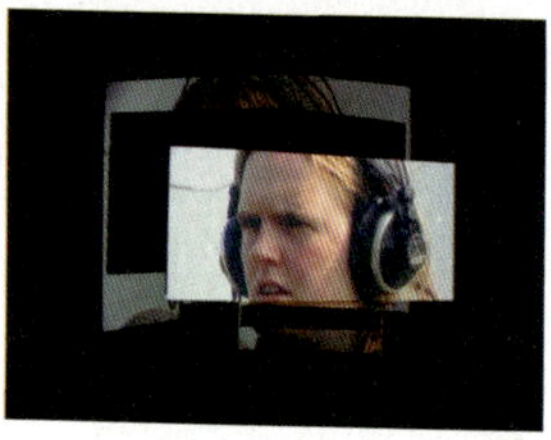

The Time Surgeon

The physical projection of video in a sculptural manner, involving a deliberate fragmentation of the image, was a distinctive feature of Mellors' video installations from *Black Gold* (2001) to *The Time Surgeon* (2007).

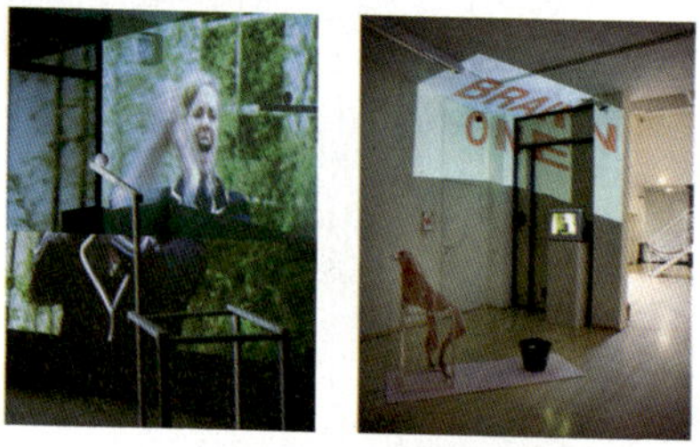

fragmentation of video in Hateball

11. Editorialising protagonists also feature as characters in the early single screen work *Pod War (The Landscape Critics)* (2002) – these 'critics' are suffering and dying in the landscape they pertain to critique; 'I am shitting myself out' etc.

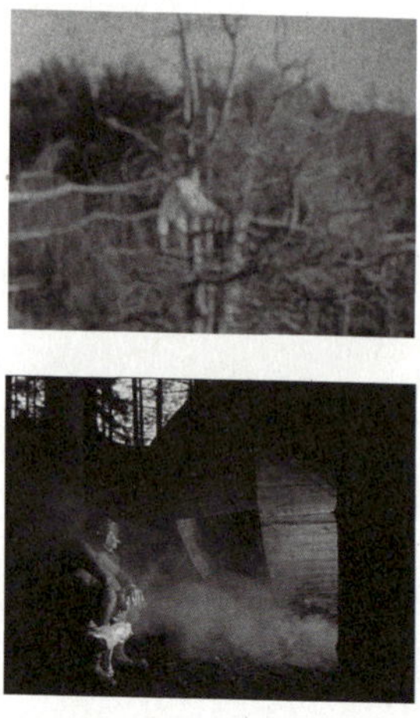

David Birkin (top) and Barney Mellors (bottom) as Landscape Critics

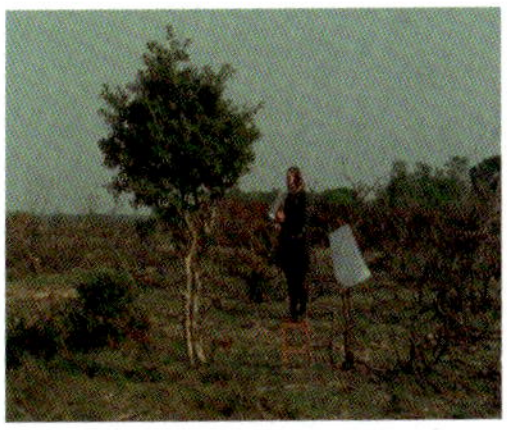

Holly Walsh as The Introduction in The Time Surgeon

The idea continues in *The Time Surgeon*, where The Introduction (played by Holly Walsh) describes herself as a disembodied entity becoming aware of her existence in a landscape emerging as a result of the words she can hear. These words are spoken by The Time Surgeon, her torturer.

12. A reference to an image of Orwell in a work

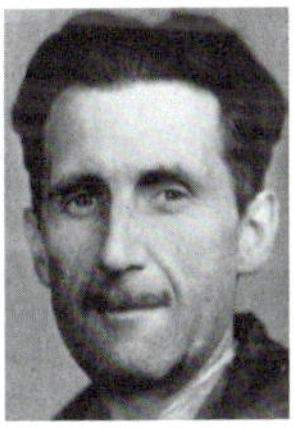

George Orwell

by Mellors and also Wyndham Lewis' *The Apes of God.*

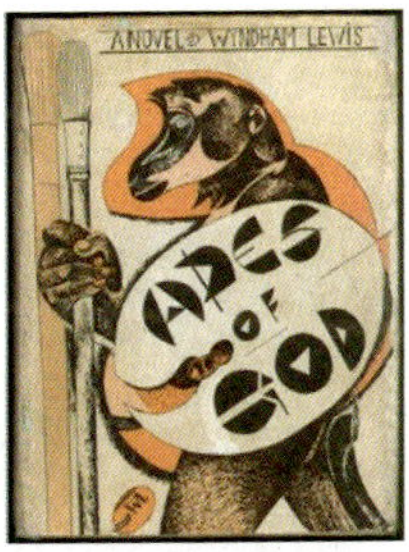

Wyndham Lewis' The Apes of God

Mellors' image may have sustained the addition of some Rice Krispies. [12A]

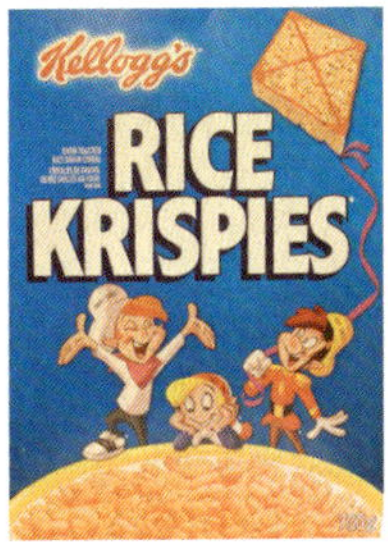

Rice Krispies

13. *The 7 Ages of Britain Teaser*, 2010. UK broadcast 21st March 2010, BBC One.[13A]

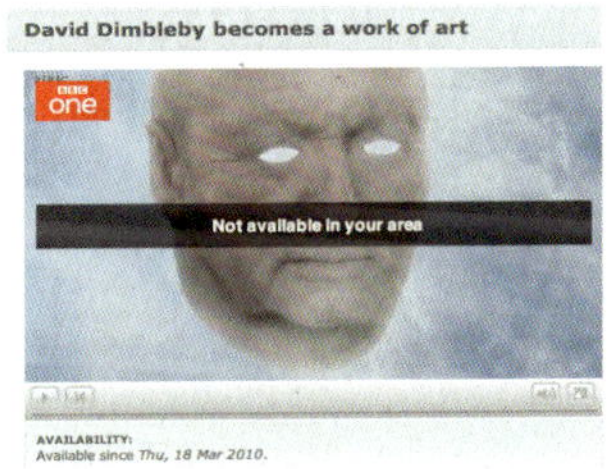

The 7 Ages of Britain Teaser on the BBC website

14. From Grizedale Arts website: Nathaniel developed a body of work that was exhibited at The Changing Room Gallery, Stirling, 5 April–24 May; The Turnpike Gallery, Leigh, 14 June–26 July; The Brewery Gallery, Kendal, 3–31st August 2003. The show was called *Prince Lightning – The Long Scratch* and comprised photographs, music and a sculptural installation. Prince Lightning is a rap-star for the British countryside.[14A]

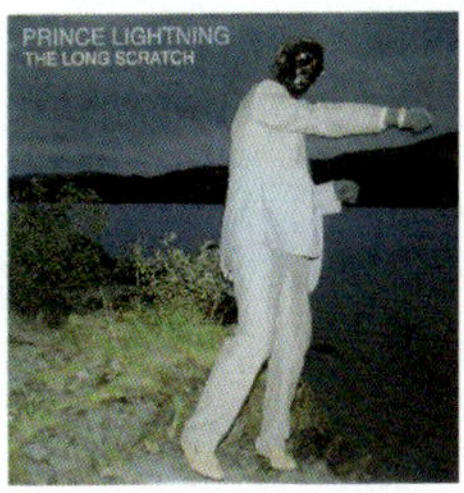

Prince Lightning – The Long Scratch, LP

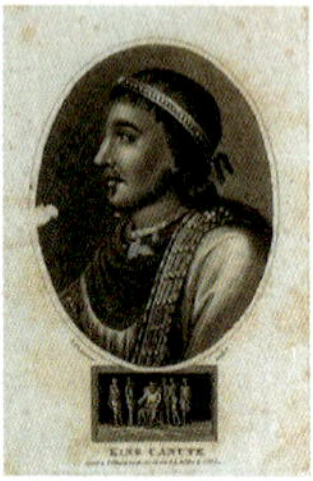

Cnut the Great

15. Cnut the Great (Old English: Cnūt; Old Norse: Knūtr inn rīki; Danish: Knud den Store or Knud II c. 985 or 995 – 12 November 1035), also known as Canute or Knut, was a Viking king of Denmark (Cnut II), England, Norway and parts of Sweden. As a statesman, with notable successes in politics and the military, and the importance of his legacy – if now obscure – Cnut seems to have been one of the greatest figures of medieval Europe. Until recently though, after the death of his heirs within a decade of his own and the Norman conquest of England in 1066, his achievements were largely lost to history.

16. King Crimson. The dynamic of this 'prog rock' group is similar to Mellors' tyrannical urge to achieve perfection: 'Between 1970 and 1971, King Crimson was an unstable band with many personnel changes and disjunctions between studio and live sound as the band explored elements of jazz, funk and classical chamber music. This period has subsequently been referred to as the "interregnum" – a nickname implying that the 'King'

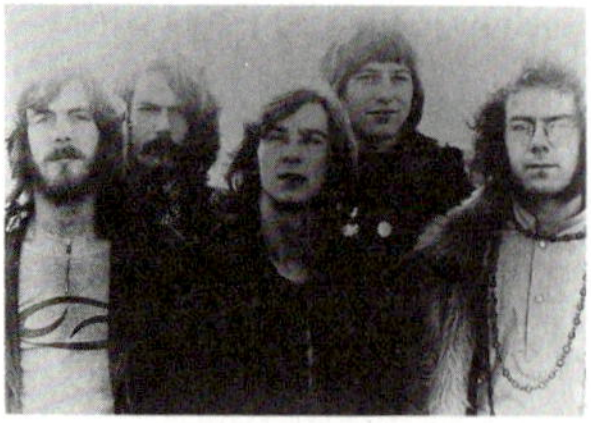

King Crimson

was not properly in place during this time. In retrospect, this interruption in career momentum can also be seen as the reason why King Crimson never attained the commercial heights of Genesis, Yes or Emerson, Lake & Palmer.'

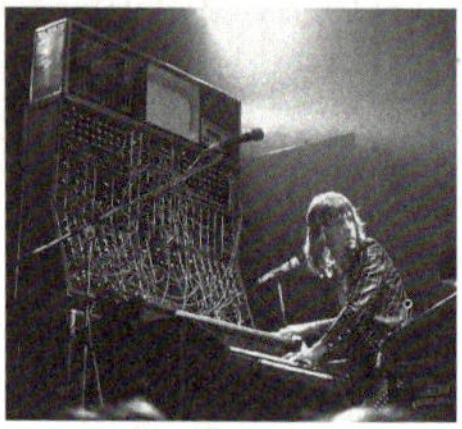

Keith Emerson at the big, modular Moog

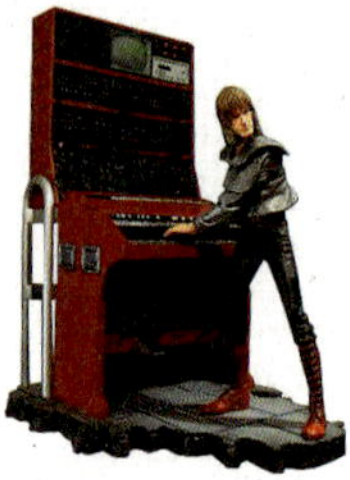

Model of Keith Emerson at the big, modular Moog

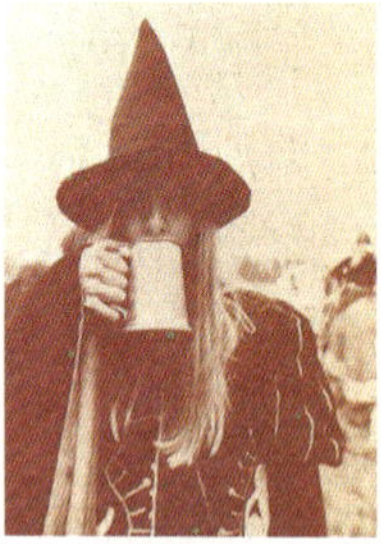

Rick Wakeman of Yes

17. King Kadmus was credited by the Greeks with the introduction of the original alphabet, or Phoenician alphabet (*phoinikeia grammata*).

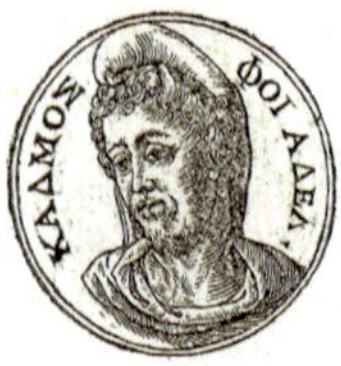

Cadmus or Kadmos in Greek, Roman and Phoenician mythologies, was a Phoenician prince, the son of king Agenor and Queen Telephassa of Tyre and the brother of Phoenix, Cilix and Europa.

In Marshall McLuhan's work *The Gutenberg Galaxy: The Making of Typographic Man* (University of Toronto Press, 1962)

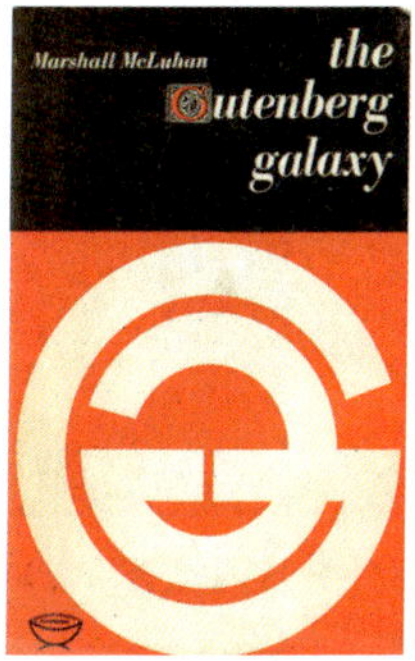

The Gutenberg Galaxy: The Making of Typographic Man'
(University of Toronto Press, 1962)

McLuhan describes the phonetic alphabetic as a colonising technology, capable of taking over other more experientially and contextually specific forms of communication, and therefore particularly suited to imperialistic, administrative cultures. The barbarian-dwarf character in Mellors' *The 7 Ages of Britain Teaser* (2010) *See* NOTE 13 is a Kadmus (Johnny Vivash) preoccupied with the word 'hammer.' 'Hammer! Hammer! Kadmus smash face with hammer!' is his response when The Operator (Gwendoline Christie) asks for his help with 'The Face' – a silicon prosthesis of David Dimbleby's face.

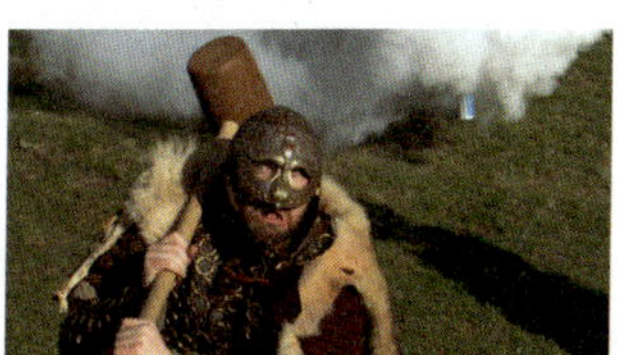

Kadmus smash face with hammer!

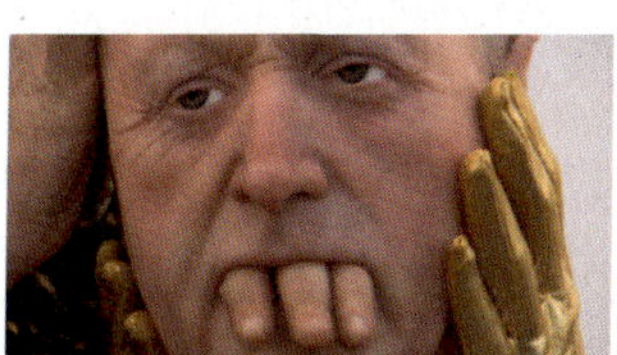

The Operator & Kadmus lose control of The Face

18. 'One reason that *Histoire de l'oeil* and *Madame Edwarda* make such a strong and unsettling impression is that Bataille understood more clearly than any other writer I know of that what pornography is really about, ultimately, isn't sex but death. I am not suggesting that every pornographic work speaks, either overtly or covertly, of death. Only works dealing with that specific and sharpest inflection of the themes of lust, 'the obscene', do. It's toward the gratifications of death, succeeding and surpassing those of eros, that every truly obscene quest tends.' Susan Sontag in 'The Pornographic Imagination', *Styles of Radical Will* (New York: Picador, 1969).

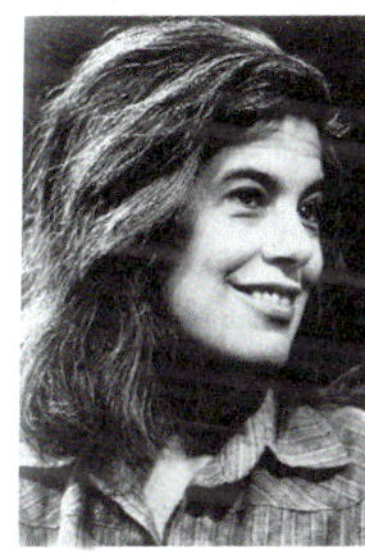

Susan Sontag

1A *Wonderlane* is a 'psych' concept album by *Captain Techworm*.

Captain Techworm were formed when bass player Reggie 'Big Sticks' Watkins and lead guitarist Dan Wolf defected from 'beat' group *Ronnie and the Rattles*. Inspired by a deep concern for the environment the two joined forces with drummer Mickey Michael and vocalist Douglas Malone to create their ecologically themed debut album. A sprawling double disc package, did produce an underground hit in *People Prepare* but subsequently sunk without trace as the costs associated with the gold foil cover featuring a snorting dragon enveloping the earth proved prohibitively expensive. With *Wonderlane* the group had streamlined their sound and with the addition of the compositional talents of keyboard player Dougie 'Keys' Kerrin the group hit their stride. The album was released in September 1969 and sold modestly but compared to the unmitigated disaster of their first long-player it was sufficiently commercial to be the impetus for their sell-out *Sidney's Dreaming* tour of 1969/1970. Popular songs such as *Congratulate the Dolphin* and *Plough* were accompanied by a huge light show and a procession of actors in themed make-up. The success was, however, short-lived. In a stopover in Australia Reggie was killed in a hotrod accident. With one of the founder members gone the group decided, out of respect for their fallen band mate, that they should retire the name *Captain Techworm*. The remaining members failed to complete the last album under the *Techworm* moniker and eventually drifted apart. Both Michaels and Malone continue to be involved in the music industry, the former particularly renowned for his work on *Pac-Man*.

1B The act of taking old bed sheets and household paint and writing slogans. The slogans are often funny and often contain dubious spelling and/or some letters painted back to front in the excited haste that accompanies their creation. 'WE HAD SOL BUT HE'S NOT A SOLDIER', the banner stated, confusingly. Mellors' face could be seen on the news reports as he watched the '90 minute display of bravura vanity'.[1BB]

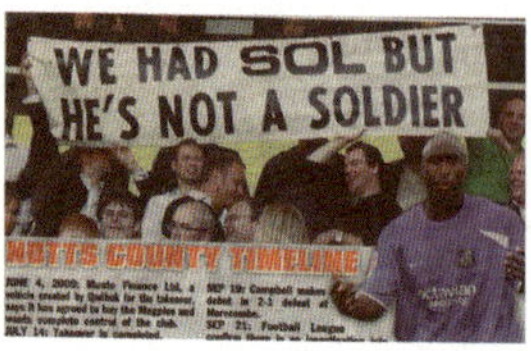

Julian Morris with banner

1C The former environs of Arsenal FC was Highbury in London. In Highbury was a popular ethnic fast food eatery existed (it has since ceased trading) called Zorba The Giant Mastiff the Biggest Dog in the World.[1CC]

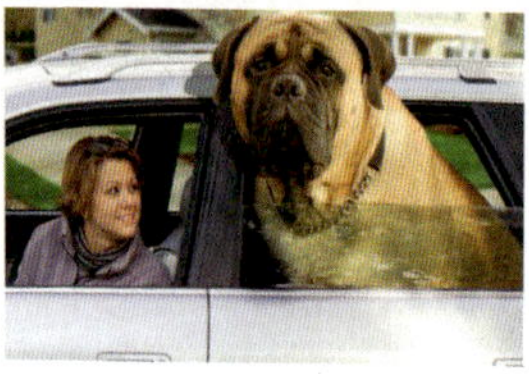

Zorba the Giant Mastiff

2A Brian plays The Object in *Ourhouse*, [2AA] 'not a character but an inhabiting entity.'

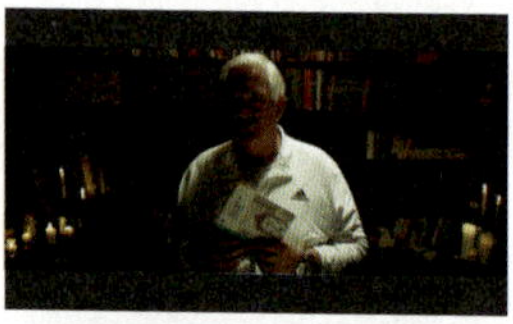

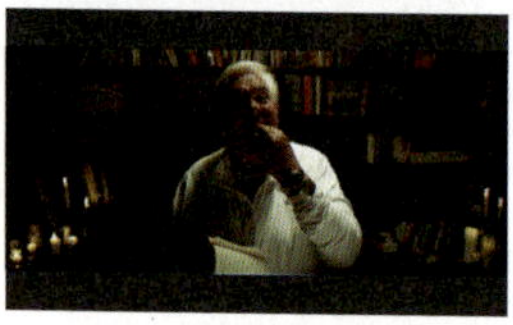

Brian Catling as 'The Object', eating books in Ourhouse

3A Now some desirable apartment finished in a vomit coloured brick situated close to the canal towpath.

3B These objects were (in no particular order)

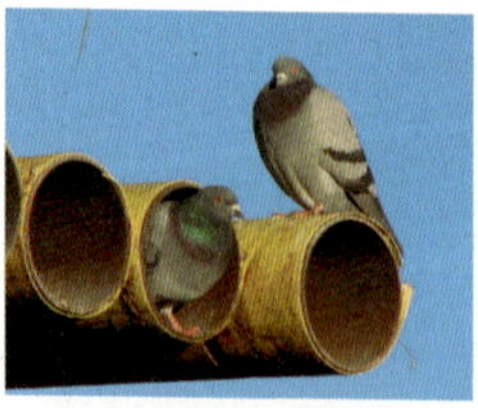

The Feral Rock Pigeon

The Feral Rock Pigeon, breadcrumbs, exhausts, plastic crates, a car bonnet, various parts of the car manufacturing process, newspapers, ancient dried feral rock pigeon faeces and fresh feral rock pigeon faeces. In this enterprise Nathaniel Mellors was assisted by Tom Woolner.

4A Mellors has owned two so called 'flight cases' both of which have required running repairs on tour. One of them was purchased with 'keep music live' stickers already applied. Apparently this is part of a long tradition of the flight-case broadcasting, 'an opinionated and unreasonable ideology in advance of its owner.' [4AA]

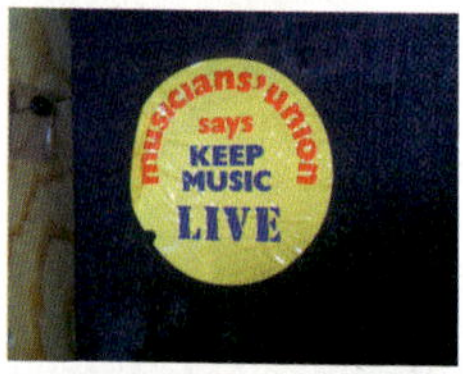

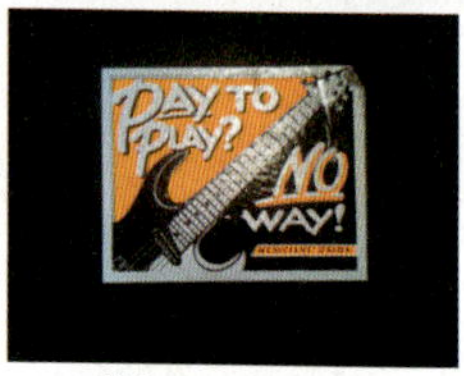

Flight cases with stickers

5A The 'skinsuit' (not to be confused with 'birthday suit') was first worn by Johnny Vivash in *First Blood No.6*

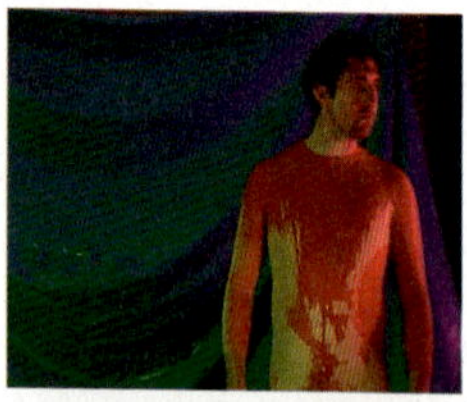

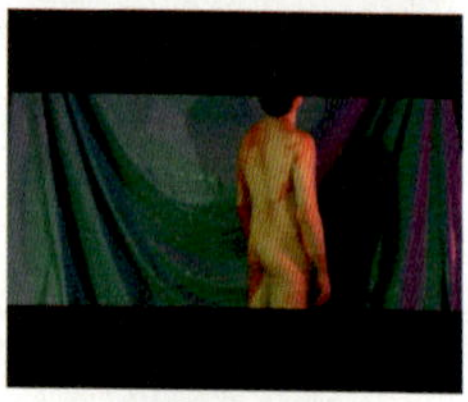

Johnny Vivash in First Blood No.6 (top & bottom)

which was part of *Hateball* in 2005. John Miller, proprietor of Las Meninas tapas restaurant, Koenji, Tokyo, next wore it. He performed Tokyo Rambo in Autumn 2006.

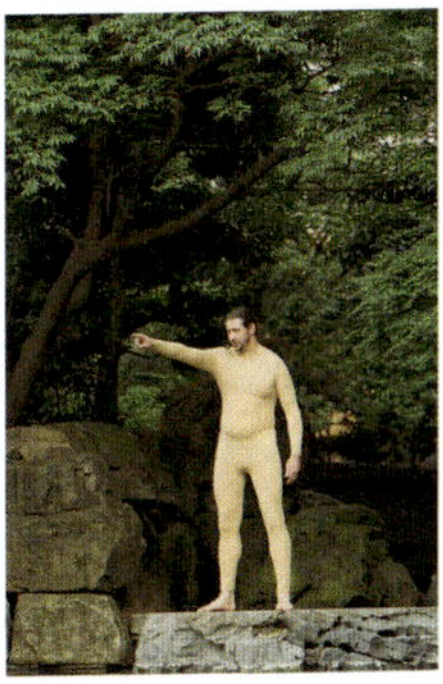

John Miller in flesh-tone unitard in Tokyo Rambo

Furthermore Bob Parks wore a skinsuit in *Giantbum* in scenes since deleted.

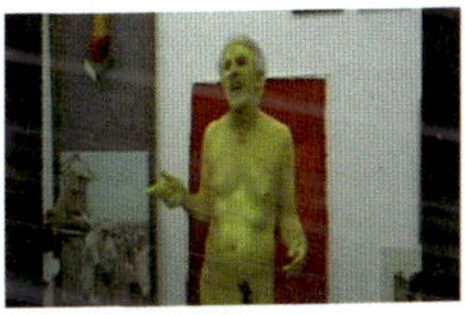

Bob Parks peforming Bignose at ZINGERpresents 6 September, 2008

Other less notable instances (as the suits were either not flesh coloured or else were hidden under other clothing) also in *Giantbum* were David Birkin as The Truthcurator [5AA]

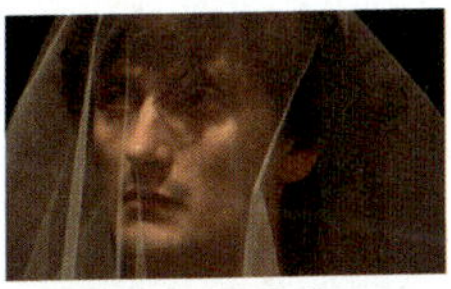

David Birkin as The Truthcurator

(wearing a white one) and Sir Boss (played by Gwendoline Christie [5AB])

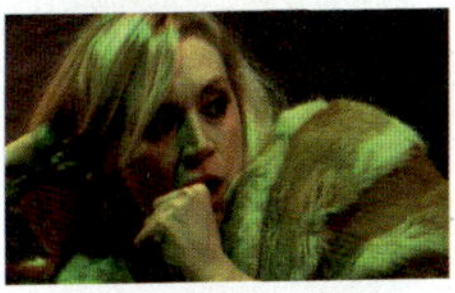

Gwendoline Christie as Sir Boss

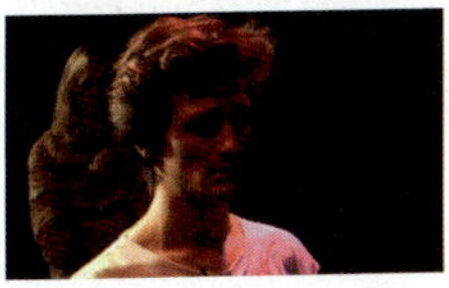

The Truthcurator & Sir Boss

who wore it under a large fur coat. The Father, (played by Johnny Vivash) wore a full white body stocking with Puma tracksuit top and white tennis shorts.

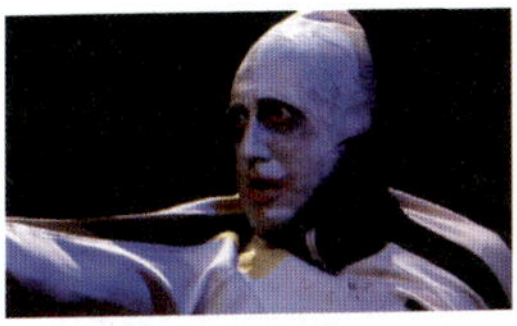

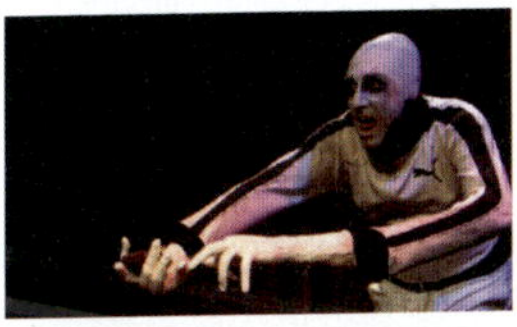

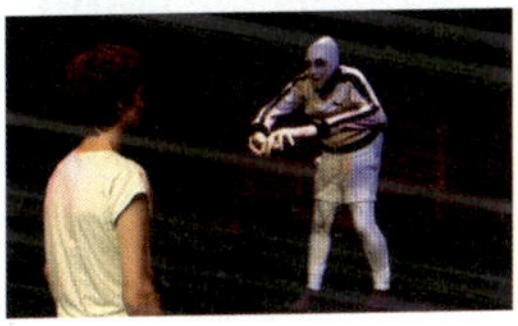

The Father in white unitard under sportswear (top, middle and bottom)

7A *The Inside vs. The Outside* – confusion between and/or conflation of these states is a running theme in the works *The Time Surgeon*, *Giantbum* (*see* **PAGE 21**) and *Ourhouse*.

In *The Time Surgeon* the Time Surgeon's 'Victim' is sent forwards and backwards in time – appearing at Oberammergau and witnessing a staging of the Passion ('These actors are *budding zombies*. I can see them raising the Christ-prosthetic up on his sticks.') From Oberammergau 'Victim' is projected back to the actual crucifixion at Golgotha, materialising inside the body of Christ 'by mistake' and discovering 'a smaller chap with a smaller book' there called Chris – a conjoined twin with an abortive script -'actually it's more of a pamphlet' - that 'contains the answers to all the worldly problems'. In *Giantbum* The Father's coprophagous claim is that the group is not lost inside the body of a Giant, but inside the bowels of God. In *Ourhouse* the pub, theatre and a municipal pool are all internal locations. These expand as The Object takes over the environment until eventually entire landscapes (desert, jungle, frozen wasteland) have to be navigated inside the house.

7B

He waved his cyst-ridden fist at the skies
And prayed for a tiny film star.
With a pole.
To dance gymnastics his way
Upon and over his weary arms
Today: miniature, her version one:
Tiny skin-based Kevin Bacon
Gives gymnastic skin-magic, magic skin
Pole vaulting from cell to cell
Healing the cuticles
and killing all the worms
A tiny versioned son of someone
Tremors going on for ever
Out of his epidermis
Through the wallpaper
Scuttling the floorboards
Walking the floor
Onto the street
Into the dirt
Picked up through the smog
Into the air
Over the hills
Atmospheric explosion
Atmospheric explosion
And return to point of contact
son of the stars
son of the stars
Tremors: going on for ever.
Tremors: going on for ever.

Excerpt, *Lab 75* (2004)

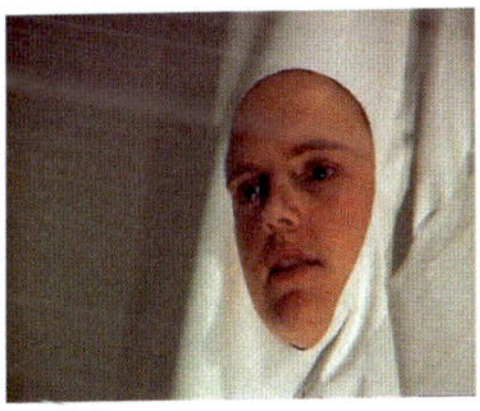

Holly Walsh as a plastic, poem-reading mountain in Lab 75

7C *The Lowry Block*. (2007) – transcript excerpt :

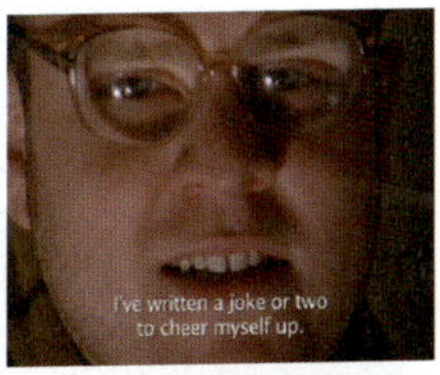

Barney Mellors as Lowry, joking in The Lowry Block

'I have written a joke or two to cheer myself up. I've made them a bit controversial, you know – to keep them modern. Here's one:
It's really depressing around here I tell thee. I've written a joke about it,

you know, “my bad luck & misery”. I’m so unlucky, so unlucky, that the first child – sorry not child – under-aged girl I had sex with gave me AIDS. It’s really depressing around here I tell thee. I’ve written a joke about it, you know, “my bad luck & misery”. I’m so unlucky, so unlucky, that the first child - it’s really depressing around here I tell thee. I’ve written a joke about it, you know, “my bad luck & misery”. I’m so unlucky, so unlucky, that the first child, no, sorry, not child, under-aged girl, I had sex with, gave me AIDS. <pause>. Gave me AIDS. It’s really depressing around here I tell thee. I’ve written a joke about it, you know, “my bad luck & misery”. I’m so unlucky, so unlucky, that the first child – no not child – underaged girl I had sex with gave me AIDS. She was a lovely girl. Lovely big flat face. But she had the AIDS, y’know. I’m so unlucky since I’ve been in Berwick I’ve caught AIDS twice. I’m so unlucky since I’ve been in Berwick I’ve caught AIDS twice. The 2nd time was with a little Palestinian lad. He was a *suicide bummer.*

D’ya get it? No. No. It’s not funny is it – because you can’t catch AIDS twice. I’ll have to re-write it. The 2nd time was with a little Palestinian lad. He was a suicide bummer. D’ya get it? No. No. You can’t catch AIDS twice, can ya? I’ll have to re-write it. The 2nd time was with this little Palestinian lad! He was a *suicide bummer.* Do you get it? No, no, it’s not funny is it. Because you can’t catch AIDS twice. I’ll have to re-write it.

I’ve got another joke! It just came to me as I was looking out into the sea. Right.

Why can there be no poetry after the holocaust?

Because it’s a really difficult word to rhyme.

I’ve got another joke! It just came to me as I was looking out into the sea. Right. *Why can there be no poetry after the holocaust?* Because it’s a hard word to rhyme. Is that good?

No? Oh, OK. I’ll rewrite it.
I’ll rewrite it.’

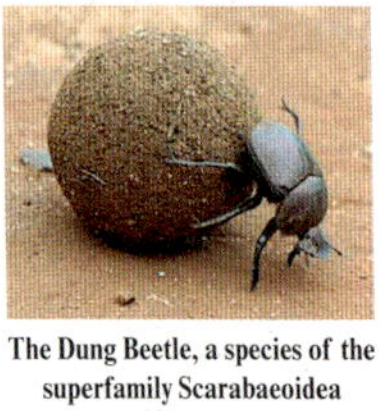

The Dung Beetle, a species of the superfamily Scarabaeoidea

8A The discussion of the dream continued thus: ‘In the dream the snake is after my scarabs. I am desperately trying to protect them. In reality I have tried hard to *unpick*, to *disentangle* – some meaning from this dream. I can only frame it as a dream of base anxiety-class. Because in reality I collect scarabs - dung beetles. I have a number of them in my fridge. Several hundred in fact – they are breeding and I am breeding them, my “Dungies”. Increasingly their maintenance requires most of my time and energy. If I seem nervous please regard this as a manifestation of concern as to my Dungies’ well-being. For their sake I must keep my observations brief and focused, to the point, concise, centred, concentrated etcetera. Today.’

9A Tape is the medium through which the Time Surgeon operates. Rain also features in the dialogue, see both the opening to The Script Writers Concept Book and this extract:

Time Surgeon: Where are you now?

Tape: <quietly> the…past.

Time Surgeon: Where abouts?
Be specific!

Tape: In…the…garden. It’s starting to rain.

Time Surgeon: What year is it? I’ll land him.

12A Provenance and usage of Rice Krispies: Rice Krispies feature as a leitmotif in *Hateball* (2005)

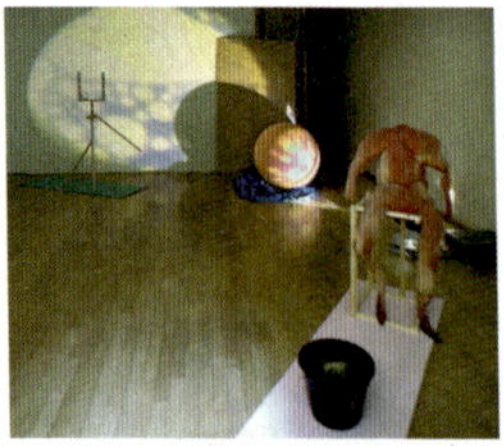

Hateball (installation detail) at De Hallen Haarlem, 2007

– this work features globules of myriad form and dimension (Kellogg’s® Rice Krispies®, gravel, earth, polystyrene balls,

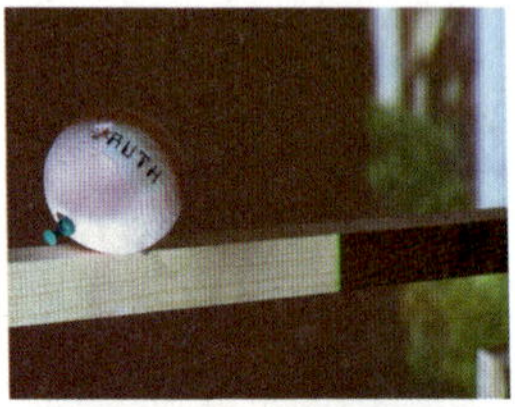

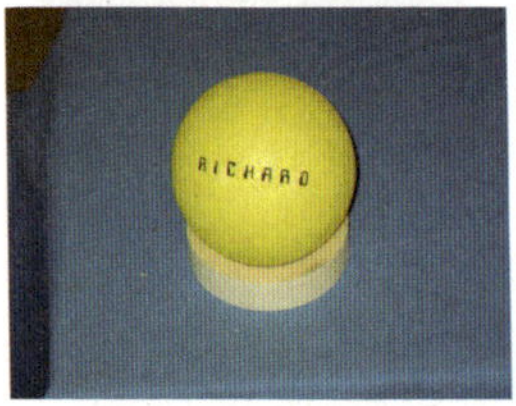

Ruth & Richard (details)

‘The Prisoner’-style weather balloon, disembodied head of ‘senile Polish Supercomputer’ *Brain One*, played by Hannah Rickards).

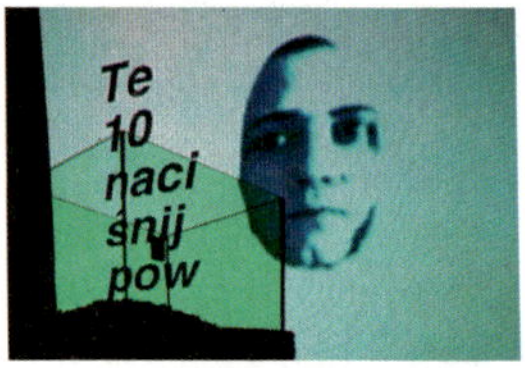

Hannah Rickards in Brain One

Rice Krispies are the most fragile and distorted type of ball in *Hateball* (2005). They are glued to the face of a glass head in a bucket that is a component of the sculptural sub-section ‘Sculpture Sculpture No.6 No.6’

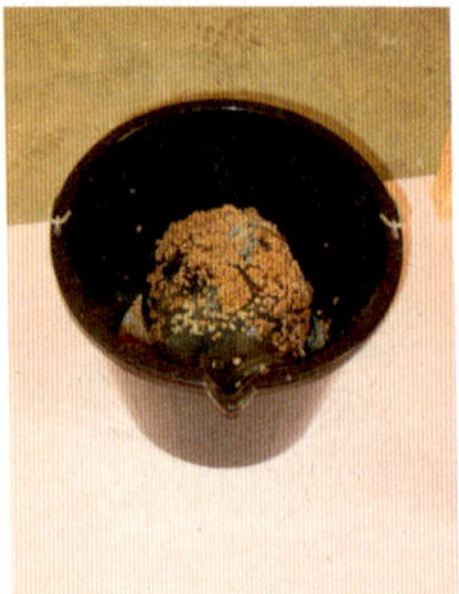

Sculpture Sculpture No.6 No.6 (detail)

‘Sculpture Sculpture’ is Mellors’ term for a mode of sculpture with an overtly self-conscious aspect as a fundamental feature, a celebration of the potential of materials to announce this reflexivity – not to be confused with contemporary mannerism.

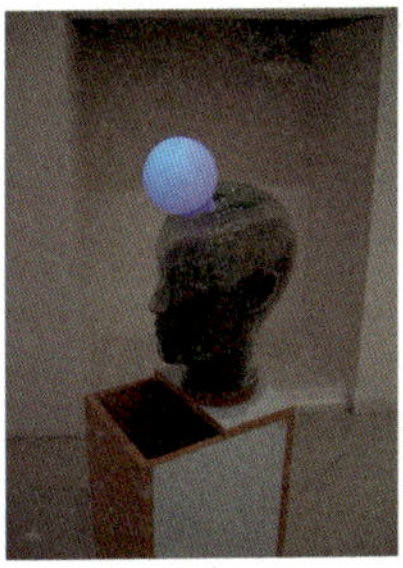

Forces of Evil (detail), glass head with earth, Rice Krispies, Blu-Tack & colour-changing ball, 2005

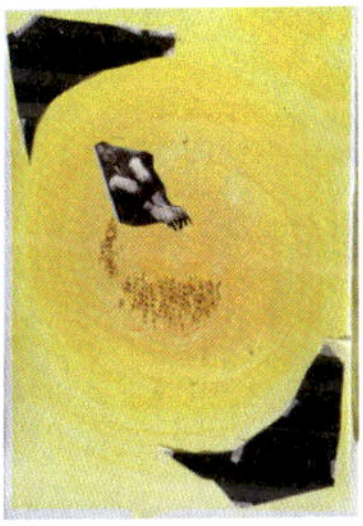

Collage Against Fear

Collage Against Fear, (2005) Paint, pencil, pen, masking tape, colour photocopy and Rice Krispies on paper, framed, featured Rice Krispies coming out of the 'bum' of a petrified man with bandaged hands swirling into a yellow vortex. [12AA]

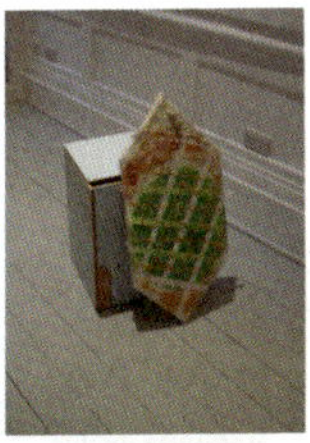

Krisskrosskrispies

Krisskrosskrispies, (2005) is a sculpture made of wood, canvas, paint and Kellogg's Rice Krispies. This work abides in a private collection in Los Angeles, the purchaser expressed conservational concerns about the work's longevity in relation to the appetite of *Periplaneta Americana* (the American cockroach) - not to be confused with the dung-beetle, which the artist identifies as a producer rather than a consumer. [12AB]

13A Reminiscent of a member of American metal band Gwar [13AA] in his dress,

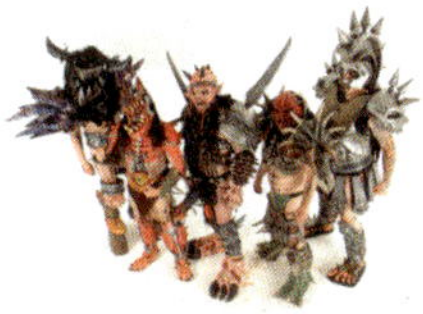

A model of Gwar

the helmeted Viking is played by Johnny Vivash.

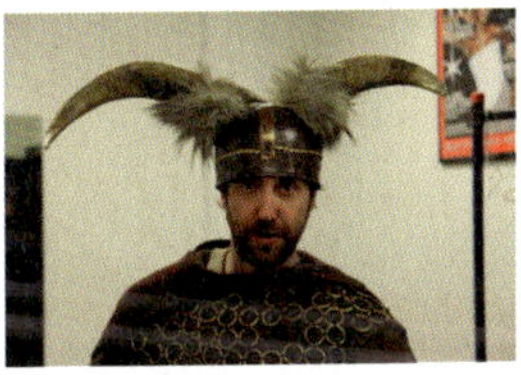

Johnny Vivash (Kadmus) incorrect helmet

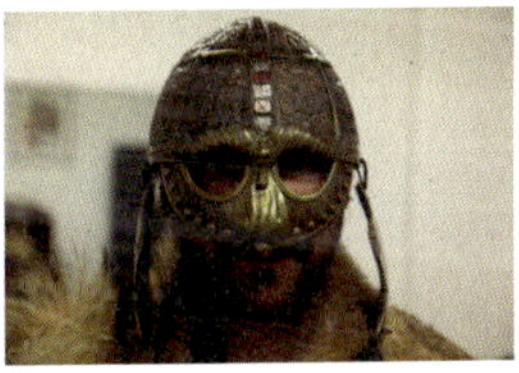

Johnny Vivash (Kadmus) correct helmet

14A Similarly motivated hip-hop artist Kool Keith created his Black Elvis

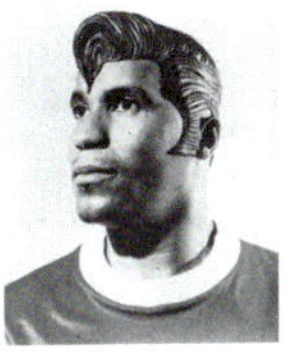

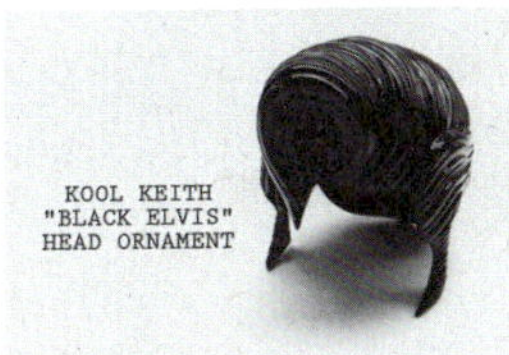

Kool Keith as Black Elvis

persona, a knowing send up of what he sees as white rock and roll excess. He described in typically esoteric style how one can play with systems of representation:

My music is black as hell. But culturally people don't even know that. They just stereotype. They look at my album cover and they're probably like, 'What's this? Is this some kind of mechanical space stuff? He looks weird. Is this Devo or something?'

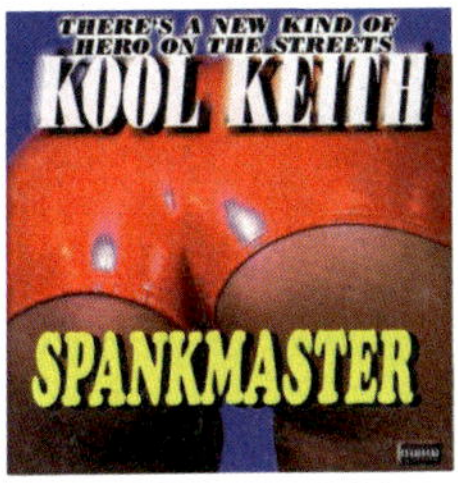

Kool Keith, Spankmaster LP, Overcore Records, 2001

1BB

Quote from Jonathan Meades' hangdog doc for BBC4. The full quote is, 'a bespoke cast of gladiatorial yob-gods, wag-roasting Croesus kids, who once a week descend from their Parnassian blingsteads to run around for 90 golden minutes of bravura vanity.'

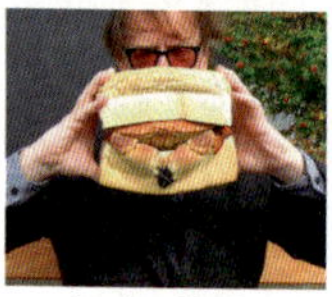

Jonathan Meades

1CC

Extract from Barnaby [1CCC] Googe's translation of Konrad Heresbach's description dated 1631 of the Bandog for the house:

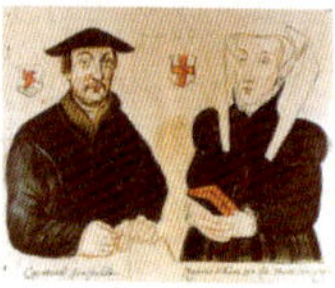

Konrad Heresbach

First, the Mastie that keepeth the house. For this purpose you must provide you such a one as hath a large and mightie body, a great shrill voyce, that both with his barking he may discover, and with his sight dismaye the theefe, yea, being not seene, with the horror of his voice put him to flight. His stature must be neither long nor short, but well set ; his head, great; his eyes, sharp and fiery, either browne or grey; his lippes, blackish, neither turning up nor hanging too much down; his mouth black and wide; his neather jaw, fat, and coming out of it on either side a fang appearing more outward than his other teeth; his upper teeth even with his neather, not hanging too much over, sharpe, and hidden with his lippes; his countenance, like a lion; his brest, great and shag hayrd; his shoulders, broad; his legges, bigge; his tayle, short; his feet, very great. His disposition must neither be too gentle nor too curst, that he neither faune upon a theefe nor flee upon his friends; very waking; no gadder abroad, nor lavish of his mouth, barking without cause; neither maketh it any matter though he be not swifte, for he is but to fight at home, and to give warning of the enemie.

2AA

Ourhouse was conceived as 6 x 50 minute episodes – an absurdist TV series hybridising aspects of the soap, drama, sci-fi and horror genres. Mellors wrote the step-outline for the 6 episode story in 2009 in Oregon in collaboration with Dan Fox.

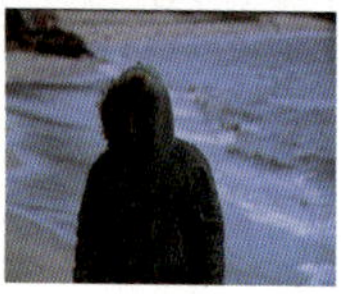

Dan Fox

Tony Grisoni performed the consultative role of 'Script Magus' during this period. Mellors has since written the script for most of the first and second episodes, as well as a few scenes from episodes three, four and five. The increasingly fantastical nature of the story presents some challenges for the future realisation and completion of the work. It is Mellors intention to complete the work at all costs, no matter how physically, psychologically or financially ruinous.

4AA

Mellors has toured with *Skill 7 Stamina 12*. In a typical anecdote he describes flying from Heathrow at 10am to LA on the morning after the opening of his *Hateball* project at Alison Jacques. Demonstrating the key attributes of any musician he was leaving behind some relationship problems that caused him to weep on the flight. The band managed to successfully play a 'gig' (according to Mellors, 'most Skill 7 gigs were good when they were not cancelled') at The Mountain for a China Arts opening curated by Maureen Paley.

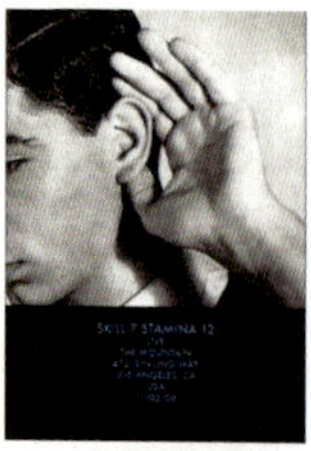

Flyer for
Skill 7 Stamina 12
gig at The Mountain

He recalls dragging his flight-case to seashore in the morning to look at the Pacific Ocean with band mate Ashley Marlowe.

5AA

On the evolution and usage of 'Truthcurator' in Mellors' work. First appearance in a two channel video installation at P.S.1 in 2005. This Truthcurator was a 'rampaging cultural monstrosity'.[5AAA] The only characteristics this truthcurator shares with the Truthcurator of *Giantbum* is his name. Truthcurator v.2 is a heroic and innocent creature. He is the prototype for the character 'Truson' in *Ourhouse*, a hybrid savant/holy fool character.[5AAB] Both are played by Mellors' friend David Birkin.

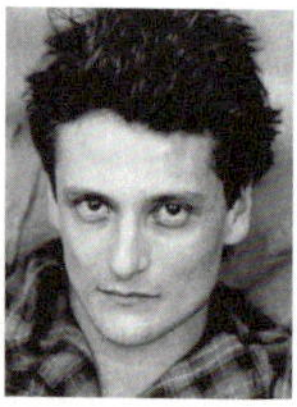

David Birkin

5AB

Along with David Birkin, Johnny Vivash and Gwendoline Christie have been key actors in Mellors' projects since 2002. Vivash is also known as 'Premiere Toy' and Christie as 'Supreme Toy' or 'Toy Number One'.[5ABA]

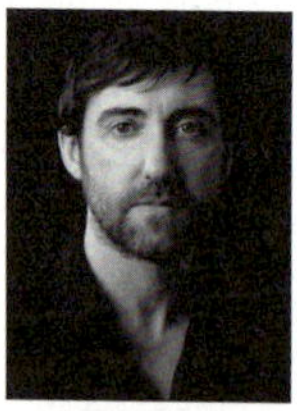

Johnny Vivash
'Premiere Toy /
Expensive Vase'

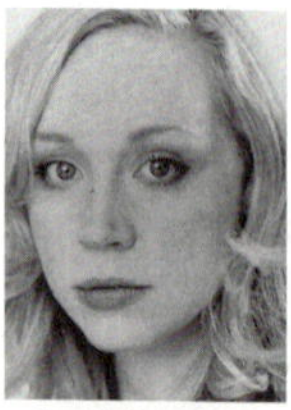

Gwendoline Christie
'Supreme Toy'

12AA

Incomplete list of works on paper:

娄里德的工厂, 涉及时间旅行和酷刑, 2006 (which roughly translates to: 'The Lou Reed Plant, Relating to Time Travel and Torture') silkscreen, pencil, yellow sand & pva on paper, sellotape, frame and foliage.

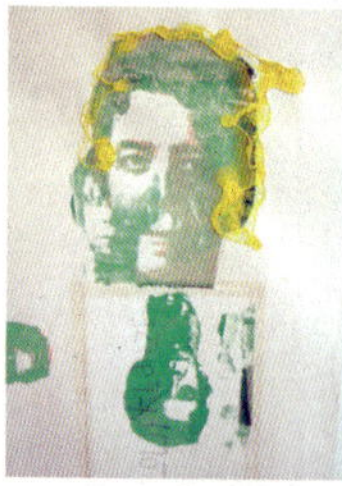

娄里德的工厂,
涉及时间旅行和酷刑

The pencilled phrase 'Loupflanze' takes the word *Urpflanze* and replaces the '*Ur-*' stem with Lou (Reed). In *The Time Surgeon* Lou Reed is used as a symbol of the artist's expanded ego

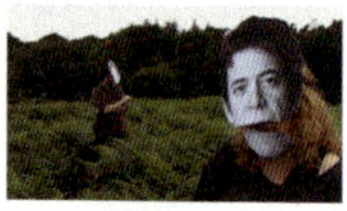

"In the future
everyone will look
like Lou Reed"

"in the future everyone will look like Lou Reed". The Time Surgeon also declares himself a fan of Goethe and becomes obsessive about finding his 'Goethe tape' which he uses to relax. Goethe's notional '*Urpflanze*' is an idea Mellors' incorporated initially as an analogue for the production of art ('*Platato's Hypothetical*

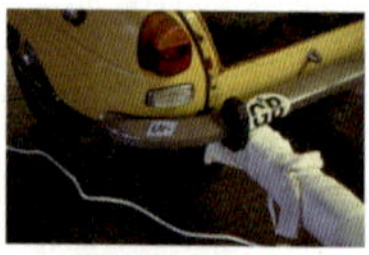

'Ur-' prefix decal in
Basic Life Support
(installation detail),
1999

Productions', 1999) and later as a fascistic political buzzword ('*MACGOOHANSOC*' - *Hateball, 2005*).[12AAA]

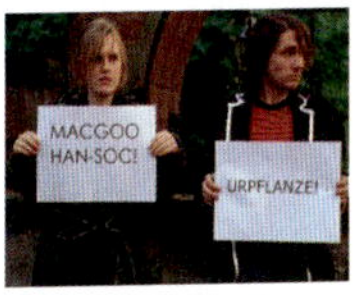

Holly Walsh and Dan Fox in MACGOOHANSOC

12AB

The voice delivering *'The Ill-Tempered Manifesto'* or *'A New Aging Manifesto'* or *'The New Old Manifesto'* was conceived as the artist's imaginary and embittered future-self. See 8A and Serpentine Gallery Manifesto Marathon (Koenig Books), pp.148-151.

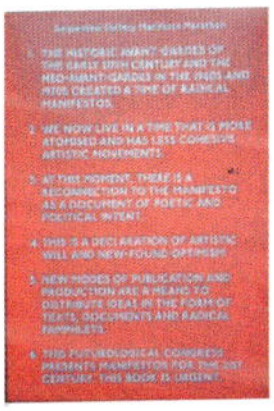

Serpentine Gallery Manifesto Marathon publication

13AA

Gwar put forward their own manifesto on television. Band members Oderus Urungus and Beefcake the Mighty were interviewed on *The Joan Rivers Show* in 1990. Like their *Jerry Springer* appearance, it was ostensibly on the topic of shock rock. Oderus and Beefcake spoke with foreign accents (Oderus - Eastern European and Beefcake - Italian) throughout the interview. Joan asked them who wrote their music to which they replied, "after we destroyed the dinosaurs, we stretched their gizzards across the Grand Canyon and Beefcake composed the first song ever." 13AAA

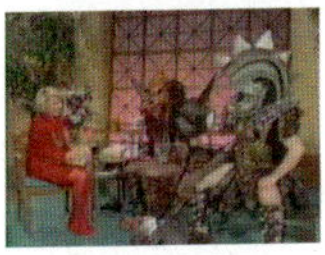

Gwar on The Joan Rivers Show

1CCC

Another notable Barnaby is one Barnaby Mellors collaborator on the Furniture Village / Jewson campaign in 2000 A.D. Barney Mellors

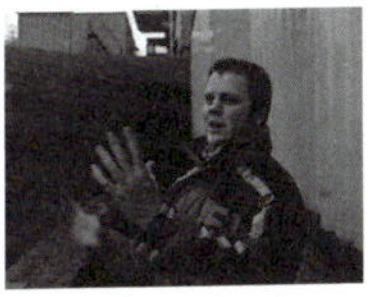

Barney Mellors improvises Furniture Village, 2000 – "a human bullet-proof crucifix"

improvised some or all of the content for a number of Mellors' video works at this time: *Furniture Village / Jewson* (2000), 'Lancaster Fishmonger Complaint' and 'Gacy'

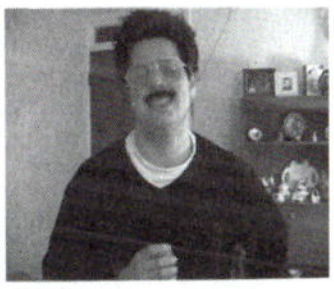

Barney Mellors improvises Lancaster Fishmonger Complaint in Black Gold

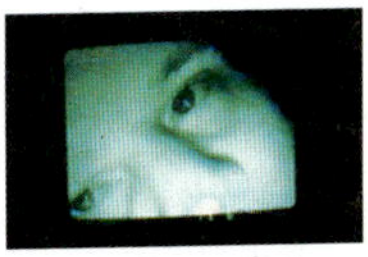

Barney Mellors improvises Gacy in Black Gold

(both from *Black Gold*, Matt's Gallery, 2001). In *The Lowry Block* (2007) Barney Mellors plays the painter L.S. Lowry.

4AAA

Also a band mate from the days of Conemelt,

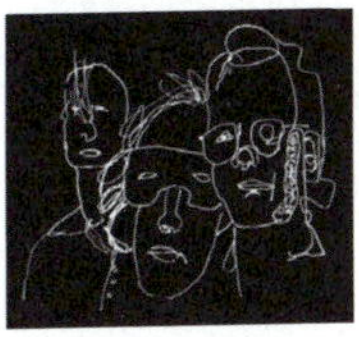

Conemelt circa 1996
L-R Grant Newman, Ashley Marlowe, Nathaniel Mellors

an electronic outfit from the Tonbridge area, UK.

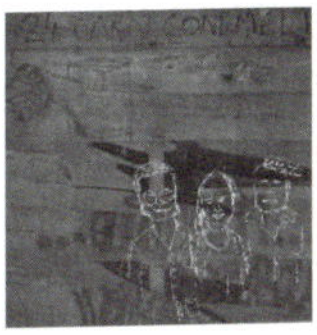

Conemelt, 24 Carat Conemelt, 1997

Conemelt travelled to gigs in different parts of Britain in Mellors' white Ford Capri, these included the Q Club, Birmingham, Herbal Tea Party, Hulme and Glasgow's The Arches. Conemelt also toured with Andrew Weatherall in an expensive and augmented tour-bus. They performed for three nights at Iceland's Tungli Club, which later burnt down (not as a result of the band's activities).

5AAA

Behold!
I have given life to this artwork
and also to this building –
splendid concrete womb of
possibility!

T*R*U*T*H*C*U*R*A*T*O*R

I am a man of the people; *curiously fashioned.*

I will explain this show and art
for you.

<Morning>
I am assailed on all sides by
small birds:
sparrows
blackbird
the 'mistle' thrush and
snipe.
They are trying to get into my bag.

The TRUTH C
URATOR

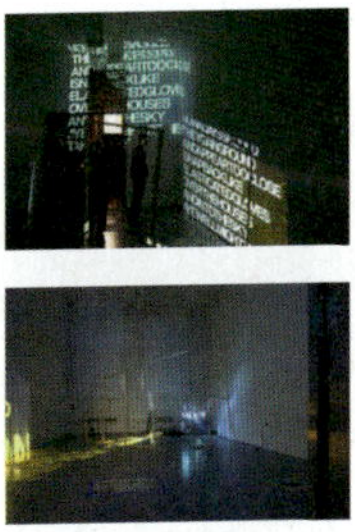

TRUTHCURATOR
2-channel video installation, P.S.1, 2004

5AAB

Simeon The Holy Fool (also known as Abba Simeon, Saint Simeon Salos or Saint Simeon Salus) was a Christian monk, hermit and saint of the sixth century A.D. He is considered to be a patron saint of all holy fools and also puppeteers.

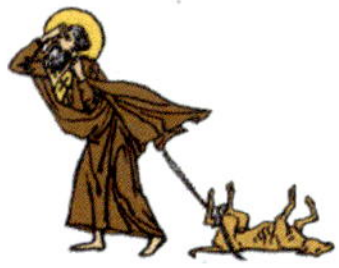

Simeon The Holy Fool, dragging a dead dog

5ABA

'Daddy's Toys.' Actors Vivash and Christie refer to Mellors at all times as 'Daddy' and themselves as 'Daddy's Toys.' Having invented these roles the toys experienced discord about the relative status of their own titles. They began to refer to themselves as 'Premiere Toy' and 'Supreme Toy' respectively. Vivash subsequently switched from 'Premiere Toy' to 'Expensive Vase.' Mellors has recently formalised his enterprise under the name DADDY'S COMPANY / MELLORFILM Ltd. The latter mis-spelling inspired by Vivash's ongoing misconception of Mellors' name.

12AAA

'I would like to reverse our "evolutionary flow", so that all of this carrion; all women and children may be re-moulded as sterile plants, devolved and revolving in space towards the uni-cellular! URPFLANZE! URPFLANZE! URPFLANZE! Beautiful garden.' (MACGOOHANSOC)

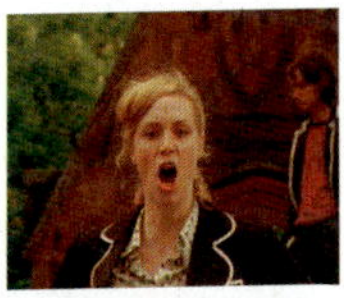

Gwendoline Christie as 'the body of Patrick McGoohan' in MACGOOHANSOC
Hateball, 2005

13AAA

http://www.junioraspirin.com/video/Gwar_on_Joan.mp4

Index

Colophon

Book A
or
MEGACOLON
or
For & Against Language

Onomatopee 44
ISBN: 978-90-78454-52-6

Text—*Nathaniel Mellors, John C. Welchman and Mick Peter*
Design—*Remco van Bladel*
Printing—*Die Keure, Bruges, Belgium*
Editing—*Xander Karskens*
Text Editing—*Vincent van Gerven Oei*
Print run—*1500*

Paper—*Reviva Print 90 gr/m²*
Typefaces—*Times New Roman, Times New Roman MT and Mercury (By Radim Peško)*

Publisher—*Onomatopee*
Bleekstraat 23
5611 VB Eindhoven
The Netherlands
www.onomatopee.net
info@onomatopee.net

This publication was made possible by—*Netherlands Fund for Visual Arts, Design and Architecture*
De Hallen Haarlem
Montehermoso, Vitoria-Gasteiz
MONITOR, Rome
Lombard-Freid Projects, New York
Galerie Diana Stigter, Amsterdam

FONDS VOOR BEELDENDE KUNSTEN VORMGEVING EN BOUWKUNST

Nathaniel Mellors would like to thank—*John C. Welchman, Mick Peter, Xander Karskens, Remco van Bladel, Freek Lomme, Vincent van Gerven Oei, Tala Madani, Karel Schampers, De Hallen Haarlem, Xabier Arakistain, Almudena Diez, Beatriz Herraez, Montehermoso, Lombard-Freid Projects, MONITOR, Matt's Gallery, Galerie Diana Stigter, Gwendoline Christie, Michael Smythe, Piera Buckland, Johnny Vivash, Andy Cooke and the Cooke family, Dan Fox, Tim Braden, Stephan Kuderna, Kees Reedijk, Martijntje Hallmann, Ansuya Blom, The Rijksakademie van Beeldende Kunsten, Hannah Rickards, Adam Sutherland, A Foundation, Grizedale Arts, Holly Walsh, Rochelle School, Bogusław Rostworowski, Tom Lauten, Robin Klassnik, Clare Fitzpatrick, Amy Botfield, Arend Nijkamp, Chris Bloor, Shirley While, Derek Horton, Joyce Cronin, Richard Bremmer, Brian Catling, Ben Wheeler, Dan Brough, Freddy Claire, Ryan Chandler, Ariel Sultan, Shaun Moan, Richardette, Lilianna Sanguino and The George and Dragon (Shoreditch), Pam Hogg, Stefan Yap, Llewellyn Thomas, Amele Sumpter, Terry Smith, Jonty Claypole, Andrea Carnevali, Alex Ellerington, Princess Julia, Tom Morton, Lisa Le Feuvre, Diana Stigter, David van Doesburg, Cristian Alexa, Paola Capata, Jelle Bouwhuis, Tony Grisoni & Oona Grimes, Pippa Brooks, Nathaniel Lee Jones, Duke Brooks, Joe Brooks, Patrick Kennedy, David Birkin, Andrew Birkin, Ned Birkin and Bee Gilbert.*